MW00776687

# SONG JOURNEY

# MARK CAWLEY

# SONG JOURNEY

A HIT SONGWRITER'S GUIDE
THROUGH THE PROCESS,
THE PERILS, AND THE PAYOFF OF
WRITING SONGS FOR A LIVING

LIONCREST
PUBLISHING

Copyright © 2019 Mark Cawley
*All rights reserved.*

Author photo by Eric Brown.

**SONG JOURNEY**
*A Hit Songwriter's Guide Through the Process,*
*the Perils, and the Payoff of Writing Songs for a Living*

Library of Congress Control Number: 2019939592

ISBN  978-1-5445-1410-9 *Hardcover*
      978-1-5445-1409-3 *Paperback*
      978-1-5445-1408-6 *Ebook*

*To my beautiful wife, Kathy, whom I've been blessed to have share this journey. You're a continual source of faith, hope, wonder, and inspiration.*

*Our daughters, Taylor and Morgan, and our growing clan, Matt, Josh, Scout, Issie, and Isla. I love you all.*

# CONTENTS

*"Without music, life is a journey through a desert."*

—PAT CONROY


*"Every day is a winding road."*

—SHERYL CROW

"A lot of people aspire to write songs. However, writing a song that conveys emotion, story, and structure is nothing short of art. On top of that, to make it 'catchy' or 'pop' or whatever area you are working in requires a whole different talent. It is becoming harder and harder to succeed in this field and having expert guidance is a godsend. Mark ticks all the boxes required as a hit writer. He has succeeded with some of the biggest artists around and has experienced all that the music industry can throw at someone, good and bad. This is invaluable experience. Mark has been, and will always remain, a major influence on my life."

—ELIOT KENNEDY,
*Ivor Novello winner, Grammy- and Golden Globes-nominated songwriter/producer; Sheffield, England*


"Mark Cawley is one of my favorite songwriters on the planet. I'm pleased to say we've been writing songs together for about fifteen years, a few I've recorded and have been blessed to have other wonderful artists record them as well. The best I can say is that it's my honor to call him one of my best friends. I enjoy writing with Mark because he comes from a very soulful place of creativity. That's what first caught my ear as I passed by a room where he was working on a tune during a songwriting summit at a castle in southern France, where we first met. Ever since then, we have written some of my favorite songs together."

—BRENDA RUSSELL,
*Grammy-nominated artist; singer, songwriter, and co-writer of the Tony and Grammy-winning Broadway musical* The Color Purple; *Austin, TX*

*"I have known Mark for about fifteen years. I would be hard pressed to find someone who possesses an entrepreneurial spirit combined with a great mentoring gift equal to his. He is truly a great man of character."*

—**CHRIS OGELSBY**,
*VP, creative for the BMG Chrysalis; Nashville, TN*

*"I have known and worked with Mark for over twenty-five years and have always been impressed by his skills as a songwriter/ musician, his humour and humility, and most of all, the fact that he is about as good a human being as you are likely to meet in any walk of life, let alone the music business! The world would be less of a place without Mark in it. I wish he lived near me!"*

—**KIPPER**,
*Grammy-winning producer (Sting), songwriter, musician and programmer; London, England*

*"Mark Cawley is a great mentor. He not only gives great feedback on material he hears, but also constructive ways to make it better and more accessible. I would highly recommend him as a songwriting coach!"*

—**IAN CROMBIE**,
*executive director of West Coast Songwriters; Palo Alto, CA*

*"I first met Mark over thirty years ago. He was the bass player and one of the principal songwriters in a regional band called the Faith Band. When I came on board with the band, Mark was one of the first to welcome me in. He always made me feel I was an important part of the group. When it came time for me to move on and seek new opportunities, Mark again was the first to encourage me to take the chance and opportunity available to me. Frankly, that transition was a springboard to where I am today—working at the top of the industry, mixing music that matters. He has always been a huge supporter of my work and a great source of encouragement."*

**—JOHN COOPER,**
*front of house engineer (Bruce Springsteen, Ringo Starr, Wynonna Judd); Brown County, IN*

*"It's rare to meet a songwriter with a proven track record of writing hit songs who also has the gift of being able to articulate to others the techniques behind the hits. Mark Cawley's ability as a songwriter is purely inspirational and his selfless and almost zen-like approach to coaching others makes him one in a million. The workshop he did for us in London blew everyone away, especially me! A font of priceless knowledge and one of life's good guys!"*

**—MARTIN SUTTON,**
*The Songwriting Academy; London, England*

# FOREWORD

*Song Journey*

I LOVE THIS BOOK!—IT'S WRITTEN LIKE A HIT SONG . . .

it's full of hooks . . .

it's to the point . . .

it's entertaining . . .

and it goes well with red wine.

My dear friend and brilliant songwriting partner, Mark Cawley, has written a how-to book for songwriters that is actually FUN to read! He's worked with and written for some legendary artists.

(Some alternative facts about them might be in the book too . . . I don't know . . . you decide.)

Mark and I have been writing songs together since the first day we met, almost twenty-five years ago. Mark is responsible for hours of mind-numbing laughter . . . Oh, and yes, some of the best songs I've ever been a part of. (Note: laughter and songwriting go well together.)

Like every songwriter, we've all been asked the same question more than once . . .

"How do you write a song?"

The easy answer is, "I don't really know," and that might be the most honest one.

But at some point, Mark thought about it . . . and then, he thought about it . . . A LOT.

Let me just say that Mark set out to answer that question . . . and more.

So . . . with the same passion he brings to everything he does, Mark was ALL IN!

He realized he had to ask and answer the question for himself.

"How *do* I write a song?" Well, he broke it down—the hits and misses.

He examined the creative process . . .

- What kind of tools are useful when your melodies or lyrics get stuck in the same ruts?

- What do you need to jump-start your dead battery?
- How do you locate your navigation system?

ON AND ON . . . You get the picture. It's a journey.

As a result of his search for what is and isn't out there for aspiring songwriters, Mark developed his own method of teaching.

You'll find that Mark has explored and subsequently mapped out some top-ten routes to a well-written song. Or, as he likes to call it, Happy Town.

On the Road Again:

Mark has already coached thousands of songwriters in person, online, over the phone, and in workshops all over the world.

I have met some of his longtime students. They tell me Mark is the best thing that ever happened to their writing. They say they love the way he teaches.

And, no surprise to me, they love what a really good guy he is.

That's my favorite part.

AND NOW, THE NEXT STEP:

*SONG JOURNEY* . . . the book.

It's conversational. Mark teaches with lots of inside stories and tips that stick with you.

You'll learn how to get your song going . . . how to keep it going.

You'll see what "next steps" you might want to take once your song is finished.

It's all neatly packed . . . from rhymes and chords to publishers and pros, Mark has supplied the maps and tools . . .

I think you're gonna love it.

It's something you can take with you.

Enjoy the ride.

—**KYE FLEMING**
*Inducted in 2009 into the Nashville Songwriters Hall of Fame*
*Three-time BMI songwriter of the year: country/pop*
*BMI country song of the year*
*Multiple Grammy, CMA, ACM, and Dove nominations*

# INTRODUCTION

**That's not him.**

Faith, a band I was a part of in the '70s, had one interesting ride after another, from being signed by Terry Knight of Grand Funk Railroad, to our first album cover shot by the legendary Richard Avedon, to being nationally hyped from double-page ads in *Rolling Stone* and billboards on Sunset Strip.

The hype backfired.

We lost the record deal, went back to playing in clubs, then slugged our way out to another major label deal with three albums on Mercury. We made the hit "Dancin' Shoes," headlined theaters, and opened for some amazing artists: Fleetwood Mac, The Doobie Brothers, Thin Lizzy, The Allman Brothers, REO Speedwagon, Foreigner, Hall & Oates, and on June 6, 1979, Peter Frampton in Fort Wayne, Indiana.

This was at the height of his *Frampton Comes Alive* phase. A little history here: back in the day, Peter and I looked a whole lot alike: long blond hair, short in stature, and rock star skinny.

Day of the gig, our band pulled into the parking lot of the Allen County Memorial Coliseum in our little mobile home, right behind I don't know how many beautiful Silver Eagle buses that were needed to make Frampton come alive that night. This parking area sat at the bottom of a fair-sized hill. Our job was to exit the mobile home, walk around the hill to the back entrance, and get a sound check in.

One by one, we left the mobile home until it was just me and my bass, backing out, closing the door behind me. I started to hear a hum and turned around to find it was coming from the top of the hill. I stopped to watch what I would call a mob: Frampton fans, a ton of Frampton fans. I don't mean casual Frampton fans; I mean rabid Frampton fans. A Frampton mob.

The hum got louder and louder, and en masse, the mob gathered and started down the hill. Toward me. Curiosity turned to panic as they started actually running downhill and I picked up the call, **"That's him!"**

As they got closer, I scoped out my options: try and get around them, through them, or get back into the mobile home and lock the door and pray. I tried the door, but it had locked behind me. The mob is waaaay closer now, and I'm in full panic mode when I hear, **"That's not him . . . That's NOBODY!!!"**

Imagine a group that size, flying downhill and putting on the brakes all at once. That's what I saw—one disappointed and pretty pissed-off Frampton mob coming to the realization that their hero was a zero.

I was left standing by my bass case next to the mobile home, looking at the back end of the mob. I picked up my instrument and made the long walk around the hill to the back of the coliseum. I remember thinking how scary it would be to be that famous. I don't know if I was happy to be nobody again, but I was alive. This was the first time I started considering my other options in music.

Most songwriters are behind the scenes—somebody but nobody to the general public. I had been writing songs for a while, and being a nobody started to sound better than being torn limb from limb. Slowly, I began to think of myself first and foremost as a songwriter.

You're reading this, so it's no stretch for me to call *you* a songwriter. Doesn't matter if you've never made a dime from writing, no cuts to your name, or if you've been fortunate enough to hang some hardware in your studio. If you've written a song, you're a songwriter.

Name it and claim it.

# PART 1

# THE PROCESS

**Sharing tips and tools at a Sweetwater GearFest.**

# CHAPTER 1

# TOOLS TO GET YOU ON THE ROAD

**Something I would love** to have you do before we get too far is answer these five questions. As a songwriter:

1. What do I want?
2. Why do I want it?
3. How will I get there?
4. What tools do I need?
5. Where am I now?

Try answering these now, wherever you are on your path. Be honest and be objective. The answers will reveal a lot about you as a songwriter and put you in better touch with your heart, your will, and your dream.

Understanding yourself, your motivation, and your needs is a great place to start this journey of thinking like a pro songwriter. Let's begin . . .

**Create a ritual.** Most successful writers I know have one. Legendary American choreographer Twyla Tharp said, "Having a routine is as much a part of the creative process as the lightning bolt of inspiration." In her book *The Creative Habit*, she says the key to a productive day is a morning routine that never varies. Mine has always been to write when I first get up. The world hasn't invaded yet, and your subconscious is still working like that dream co-writer. You might choose to write from 7:00 a.m. to lunch, or from 1:00 p.m. till 5:00 p.m., or all day and all night. Whatever you decide, stick to it. If this is fairly new to you, I would suggest starting with a few hours, same place, same day, same time, and then set a time to stop. In the beginning, try two hours, even if it's working well. The idea is to look forward to writing the next time. If it becomes a miserable, staring-at-a-blank-page, clock-watching experiment, you're bound to quit.

**Create a "Help-Hurt" list.** Take a piece of paper and draw a line down the middle and one across the top. In the box on the top left, write the word *Help*. On the other side, write the word *Hurt*. When you've reached the end of your writing time, take a few minutes to reflect on what helped your writing and what hurt it. It can be the smallest thing such as, "I ate too much and got sleepy," or "I decided to browse the internet," (maybe the biggest culprit). Write those things in the "Hurt" column. If it helped to get up really early and focus, put that down on the "Help" side. Over time, you'll start to see patterns. Dump the bad ones; keep the good ones. You want to replicate the good days to give yourself the best chance of writing success.

**Create a mission statement.** You've seen or heard these for companies. Life Is Good has a simple one: "To spread the power of optimism." Warby Parker, the trendy eyeglass company, has this one: "To offer designer eyewear at a revolutionary price, while leading the way for socially conscious businesses." You're not a business, but think about your goals as a songwriter. They're not easy to write, but the more you can define and distill just who you are as a writer, the better choices you tend to make. You can't be everything to everyone, so who are you? Having your own mission statement to reference along the way is a terrific tool for any songwriter. You're in the business of you, and you need to know your business.

What if you had one like this?

> **To use everything I've learned, all of my gifts and talents, to write life-affirming, uplifting songs. To never stop learning and growing as a writer.**

There's one to claim, and if you write it out and look at it from time to time, it can go a long way to keeping you on track.

You have a ritual, and you're on a mission . . . So let's start this songwriting journey together.

**Understanding yourself, your motivation, and your needs is a great place to start this journey of thinking like a pro songwriter.**

Printemps de Troubadour
Second Songwriter's Retreat

Bugle Songs
Spring Session 1993

**Miles Copeland's second castle retreat.**

# CHAPTER 2

# WHAT'S THE BIG IDEA?

What's the single biggest thing that separates a unique song from the ones that earn the dreaded "nice" comment? The idea. I've written all over the world and in lots of different genres. It always comes down to the big idea and how well you work it. The big idea and the title. I'm a title writer; I like to have an interesting title to start with, and that title should sum up my big idea.

I was part of a songwriting panel a few years back that included an A&R (Artist & Repertoire) guy. An audience member asked about the importance of a good title. The A&R guy shared a scenario about looking for a song for an established artist. He explained the process and mentioned the fifty-plus songs currently on his desk as part of that search.

**The process starts** with a call to the writers who have written the artist's past hits, followed by a call to the hot writers of the day. Somewhere in between come the songs written by various writers signed to publishing companies owned by the artist or producer and, of course, the songs co-written by the artist. Because the artist is no fool.

After all this, maybe, just maybe, there's room for ONE outside song. Something no one else has come up with. Something so unique it not only hasn't been written, but it also hasn't been imagined. THIS is the unsigned songwriter's best chance.

Keep in mind, our guy is looking for a hit single . . . *only* a hit single. It's a minor miracle the unsigned writer's song has actually made it to the desk. The A&R guy's time is valuable, and no way is he going to make it through all those fifty-plus songs sitting on his desk. Now to his big point: if he looks over the pile and spies a song called "So in Love," and another called "I Killed My Ex with His Own Axe," which one gets his attention? You guessed it.

At this point in the Q&A, more than a few writers in the audience got pissed off. "What if the love song is the best one ever?"

"Does every title need to be a gimmick?"

"This is so unfair!"

Maybe it is unfair, but he's going to play the axe song at least through the first chorus, just because he wants to know how the writer is going to pull this title off. It's intriguing. Same with book titles, movie titles, and so on. The object is to get you to open the book, see the movie, and pull you in.

You can find a million examples of hit songs with basic and even boring titles, but if we're talking about the first-time, unsigned writer, the odds go way up for it to get noticed with an interesting title—a big idea. Where do you find them?

I live in Nashville, and it's almost a given that if you're writing on

Music Row, you're probably co-writing with one or more writers, and you're going to start by talking and talking and more talking. Why? Because every writer here knows how to put a song together. It's what you're writing about that can make the difference. You might talk about what's going on in your life, the nightly news, something from your upbringing, your friends, your friends' friends. You talk until you find something fresh and, hopefully, relatable.

This last one is a biggie. Before I agree to coach a writer, I ask them about themselves, and once in a while, I will get this response: "I just write for myself; I don't care if anyone gets it or not." Well, I don't get it, and I usually don't coach them. I write songs to communicate with as many people as possible; writing about things that are relatable is a good way to start. The great poet Maya Angelou put it this way: "The idea is to write it so that people hear it and it slides through the brain and goes straight to the heart."

What if you don't have access to co-writers? I'm going to talk more about co-writing later, but one of the best things you can do is the same thing I've done since I started writing songs: look for lines and titles. These lines and titles may not always be the big idea; in fact, they might not end up as titles at all but could just end up being a line in your verse or bridge. It's a simple idea but so worth it. Here are my top three ways to find them:

1.  **Bookstores.** I know, they're getting harder to find. Libraries can work just about as well. Walk up and down every aisle. You're not looking to read a novel on this trip; you're looking to find a title that jumps out at you enough to where you'd want to pull the book down and read the

back. Don't. Just add the title to your list and stay on the
hunt. You don't need to know what a title is about, just
that it's interesting to you. I've found titles in the mater-
nity section of Barnes & Noble. Write it down and keep
moving. Same for a library. You're not stealing, you can't
copyright a title, but that's not the point. You're hunting
and gathering for another time—a time when you're fresh
out of divine inspiration.

2.  **Movies and TV.** It's all about being intentional here.
Keep something close by to write down those lines you
hear. The more you do this, the more your ear becomes
trained to pick those out.

3.  **Eavesdropping.** I wrote with Craig Wiseman for a couple
of days and had some fantastic conversations about
finding ideas. Craig is one of the most successful country
songwriters in history: "Live like You Were Dying," "The
Good Stuff," and tons more. One of his go-tos was going
to Walmart and just listening to people talk. His logic was
that the people there are the people who buy the type of
music he writes, so he writes about what they talk about.
Well, we're back to the relatability idea. He described
himself as a Walmart writer. Brilliant.

**You've no doubt** heard the idea of a writer's antenna. It should be
up all the time, tuning into anything and everything the universe
puts out there. Being hit by lightning makes for good songwriting stories, but every songwriter I know is on a constant lookout
for that big idea. Most of the time, it means digging for them
rather than expecting lightning to strike. I heard a recent interview with Rodney Crowell where he said he thinks "inspiration
is earned." Amen.

Once you have some lines and titles, make a list. Don't prioritize, don't alphabetize, don't pick favorites. Just get them all down in one place. Next time you sit down to write, pull out your list and keep it nearby. Some of those lines or titles may not turn out to be the ones you'll use for your chorus, but they might make it into a verse, pre-chorus, or a bridge. Point is, if you have written it down in the first place, then there's something about it that just begs the right setting in your lyric, and you're much better off starting with a provocative title than just writing a song to write a song without a great idea.

Guard this list with your life. Make copies, and whatever you do, don't give your list to other writers. Bring a few of your lines or titles to a co-writing session so you can pull them out when the air in the room is totally dead. But keep in mind, once you've thrown your favorite, hard-earned line out into the room and your co-writer loves it and runs with it, it's gone.

I attended a few of Miles Copeland's retreats in the South of France in the early '90s. Each day for two weeks, all the writers were grouped in threes. We had until the dinner bell to write a song. By the beginning of week two, I had a few visits from fried songwriters asking if they could get a look at my book of titles. *Just for a minute.* I get it, but NO.

The big takeaway from this is that over the long run, you can't depend on the muse showing up on time. You need those gems on your list.

Once you get your list, one of those titles is going to poke its head up. You decide to give it a go. Before you do, consider a "second concept," which is an exercise that can let your subconscious shine. Ask yourself: you have an idea and are ready to write it, but is it the best version of your idea?

I was coaching a songwriting client who had done her homework, intentionally finding some lines that might be worth considering. I asked her to read a few. A couple were OK, a few predictable. Then she said, "What about 'Thirty Seconds from Religion'?" She thought it could be about someone who's on death's doorstep and would be meeting their maker soon. Yep, I got it. But it also seemed a little predictable. Maybe relatable, but not the most upbeat idea for her lyric.

I asked her to think about another concept or angle and let me know in our next session. Not only did she come up with one, but she had a whole lyric written. This time, it was a story about a long-suffering wife whose husband is cheating on her (c'mon, it's Nashville after all), and she's had it. He used to be a God-fearing man, sat beside her at church every Sunday, but now had lost his ever-loving mind and was living like he was single. When I say she'd had it, I mean to the point of taking this guy out.

So her lyric tells the story of what he's been up to, and the chorus comes to the point. He is going to straighten up and be sitting in his usual spot next to her in church this Sunday, or he was going to the service in a pine box. Either way, he was going to be seeing his maker . . . Thirty Seconds from Religion. Great second concept and way more interesting and unique than the dying man version.

Give some thought early on to the emotion you want to convey. There is a common belief that we have six basic emotions: happiness, sadness, fear, anger, surprise, and disgust. You can find more

(I would add lust and jealousy—lots of song material there). You can label them differently (love, hate). However you make your list of emotions, pay attention to which one you're writing about. Mix too many and a listener has trouble knowing how you want them to feel.

You've worked to find that big idea and thought about it from a few angles. Now let's step on the gas.

Oh, yeah, now's a good time to kill the editor. We'll revive him later.

**❝**

**I write songs to communicate with as many people as possible; writing about things that are relatable is a good way to start.**

**❞**

**Co-writing with the awesome Sarah Buxton.**
**Franklin, Tennessee, 2002.**

# CHAPTER 3

# WRITING
# YOUR LYRIC

There is no one way to write a song. You may write melody first or mix it up, but for our purposes, let's start with writing your lyric.

What's a good place to start once you have a title or an idea of what you're going to write about? Prose. Think about the title, say it aloud . . . a bunch. What does it bring to mind? Got something? Take a few minutes and write the idea in prose. Don't rhyme, don't worry about being clever, just write a couple of lines describing what you're going to write about. Lennon and McCartney could have written, "'Penny Lane' is about the images of everyday people on the street in my town and what they mean to me."

Prose serves a couple of purposes. As you write your lyric, check your prose to see if you're still writing about one thing. Is everything supporting your idea? As you try to write, prose may reveal there's really nothing there. This has happened to me more than once, and I'm usually grateful I was saved from spending all day on a nonstarter of an idea.

**The next step** is a biggie and usually a big mistake. You begin to "write." I mean "write" in a bad way. You don't want to sound like just anybody, so you try to sound like a "writer." I always think of the famous *Saturday Night Live* skit with Jon Lovitz as the Master Thespian. Just search YouTube for a few moments, and you'll get the idea. You don't want to feel the sweat in your lyric.

Instead of jumping right in, try closing your eyes, thinking about your idea, and then writing what you see. Don't rhyme, don't worry about cadence or how cool it looks on the page, just write. If you're writing a song about meeting the love of your life, talk about the time of day, name the place you met, what the weather was like. Color of her hair. Even the smallest detail can make the difference between a generic lyric and one that comes to life. If it's a car, what's the make? These details make up the real stuff. Write the real stuff because it's the good stuff. You can make it pretty later.

Remember the editor? Still dead. What do I mean? If you begin to self-edit in the moment, it's toxic. I've mentored songwriters who have found themselves stuck simply because they were focusing on a line or an idea way too early—before they had enough on the page to even begin to think about the editing process. Write first, edit later. Much later.

Hopefully, you're filling up that page now, but once in a while, take a look at the prose you wrote earlier. Does everything in your lyric still support your prose? Does your third verse introduce a cat into the story of two people falling in lust? Hard choices, but the cat probably has to go. Again, most lyrics are about one thing. Prose can help you remember what that thing actually is.

If you have one mantra as a lyricist, let it be "Show. Don't tell."

I wish I'd invented this, but I'm not that smart. Any Nashville writer knows this truism, and it applies to every kind of lyric. If you're telling, you're just reporting. "Just the facts" is not a good idea here. You want to paint a picture, and you do that with color and detail. Make the listener see what you want them to see.

The late John Braheny wrote one of the best books on songwriting I've ever read called *The Craft and Business of Songwriting*. In it, he uses this example to illustrate the point:

Look at three objects—a car, a book, and a musical instrument:

- My great 1982 Porsche 928 with a broken right taillight.
- My paperback book with a blue cover and the words *Gift from God* printed in gold.
- My old white Telecaster with a broken B string and a missing volume knob.

Now you see 'em . . .

- My Honda
- The book I'm reading
- I play an instrument

. . . now you don't. Show; Don't tell.

So how much color and detail is too much?

I read a piece in Jimmy McDonough's biography of Neil Young, *Shakey*, in which he compared a good lyricist to a "stager." My daughter, Morgan, has her own interior design business here in Nashville and gets called in occasionally to be a stager. Her job is to look at a house that's on the market and put herself in the buyer's shoes. Is there too much of the owner's memorabilia or tchotchkes in the house? Is it too sterile? How can she make the house inviting so the buyers can not only pick up on the vibe but also actually see themselves living there? A good lyric writer does the same job—adds just enough color and detail so the listener sees what you want them to see. If there is not enough color and detail, the listener is left to only imagine.

I know you've heard a song and felt it was telling *your* story. That's good lyric writing. Too much detail and it's only the writer's story. Just enough and it becomes yours. I've never seen Penny Lane in Liverpool, England, but I've seen Hoover Avenue in Endwell, New York. "Penny Lane" made me think of my street growing up in Endwell. Color, detail, picture perfect.

Putting action in your lyric is a must. I was mentoring some writers not too long ago on a song about being fearless. The narrator wanted desperately to show strength and courage in a big way, but the last line kept falling flat. It went like this:

I wanna be fearless
I wanna be brave
I wanna . . .

Nothing. My buddy Martin Sutton is not only a great writer and mentor but also one of the funniest writers to spend a day with. He came in, listened to the problem, and offered this last line:

"I wanna run into the fire and not be saved."

Loved it. Action and a big idea.

Be very careful with using current slang as a lyric tool. It might be perfect for now, but if you hope for a long shelf life, let's hope you didn't "fax" someone in your lyric or use a term like FOMO, because your fear of missing out will be justified if someone looks at the song a year from now.

**I wrote a song** called "Dance with a Stranger" that illustrates many of the key points I make in my lyric coaching. Color, detail, creating a consistent language, action, and even putting my title search to good use. Pat Pattison's book *Writing Better Lyrics* has a terrific section on object writing, also called sensory writing. It involves writing about something without using sight. What would it taste like, smell like, feel like. His book does a much better job than I can of explaining it. Reading his work, I recognized how I had used object writing before I knew what it was.

The lyric I wrote made good use of action words. *Throw the window open* is better than *open the window*. *Grab my shoes* is better than *picked up*. The narrator's language, how they speak, is also huge.

A little background on how this song came to be: Tina Turner was at her height, and I loved her. I had been trying to land one with her for a few years when a call went out to write a single for her greatest hits. There was a time when a greatest hits package contained just the hits, but labels learned that by adding a brand-new song as a single, they could spark even more interest in the record. I was so ready for this shot. As with most major projects, there was no definitive deadline. They needed it "yesterday." I had given myself fake song assignments and fake deadlines for years. (Something I would recommend doing when you're starting out.) The first thing I did was to totally immerse myself in her records.

What did she tend to sing about? Any common keys? Range? Language? I was looking for clues.

I knew it needed to be up-tempo and dead sexy. I started with a drum loop that felt, well, sexy. Even though I'm more comfortable writing on guitar, I started on my keyboard. I'm not good, I'm not even close, but I am able to leave the (still dead) editor outside and play like a kid on keyboards. Something started to feel good. I played around with some chord changes—again more vibe than technique—and started looking for something to sing and, more to the point, something to sing about.

I began to imagine a short story. Usually, the story evolves from the title for me, but in this case, it had more to do with imagining the artist's life. However you come to this, it helps to think of a story song a bit like a book or movie. It has a beginning, middle, and end. In my story, a woman from the South (like Tina) had escaped from a bad relationship (again, like Tina) and found herself in a new town. That was all I had for a few days. I kept playing the groove and changes over and over, waiting for something to speak to me.

I looked over at the list of lines and titles I had been compiling, neatly typed out and sitting near my keyboard. I had looked it over countless times, but at that moment, I read a simple title I had written down from a book on English film. *Dance with a Stranger*. No idea what it was about, and I've still never seen the movie. It fit like Cinderella's slipper—not only matched my chorus melody but also gave me the big idea for the song.

Now my woman from the South went to New Orleans to get away from the bad romance. I had just been in New Orleans with

WRITING YOUR LYRIC    41

my family. Beautiful, strange, hot New Orleans. All my narrator wants to do is to feel a human touch. No come-ons, no relationship, no commitment—just to be held and dance with a stranger. Here's what I wrote, along with annotation of the techniques used in the lyric.

## "DANCE WITH A STRANGER"

On a warm summer evening *(detail)*
I'm dancing to the radio alone *(introduces the narrator)*
Don't need no conversation *(language—this is how the
   narrator speaks)*
Just the sound of a lonely saxophone *(object writing,
   imagery)*
Throw the window open *(action)*
Let the breeze take me away *(action)*
Ya see, I gotta lose this ol' heartache *(staying in character)*
Before the sun comes back to stay *(different way of saying
   "before sunrise")*
I've been doin' my best to forget you *(lead-in—grounds the
   lyric to draw listener in)*
But I can't do it on my own

CHORUS:
**I need to dance with a stranger** *(The big idea,
   plain and simple)*
**Hold him in my arms**
**Close my eyes, make believe he's you**
**I need to dance with a stranger**
**To take my hurt away**
**Before I'm over you**

Hear the city hummin' (*object writing, language*)
Grab my shoes and go downtown (*action*)
Won't need no invitation (*language—staying in character*)
Just to hear the sweet, sweet sound (*object writing*)
And I don't want no man to ask me (*language*)
Where you been all my lonely life? (*twisting a common
    pickup line*)
Just wanna move real slow (*action*)
And have somebody hold me tight
I've been doin' my best to forget you
But I can't do it on my own

CHORUS

BRIDGE:
I hear the heart is a lonely hunter (*mixes in a more poetic
    phrase, introduces something different; also came from my
    list of lines—famous book and movie from the '40s*)
And I believe it to be true
This heart is learning to forget
I ever fell in love with you

CHORUS

I demoed the song, and my publisher, Torquil Creevy, had the
idea to just take it in to Tina's label. They got back to us the
same day, put it on hold, and said they thought it was the perfect
single for the greatest hits. We celebrated that night and the next
day. (This is a good time to say that wasn't the best plan—don't
be racking up charges on your Visa because "It ain't final till it's
vinyl.") A couple of days later, we got the dreaded call. The hold

was released. Everybody involved thought it was a slam dunk . . . except Tina.

Soon after, I was back home and got a call from someone with a thick New York accent letting me know Taylor Dayne would be calling in a few minutes because she wanted to record "Dance with a Stranger." Taylor was on a roll in those days, so I was a happy boy again. The phone rings and another New York accent says, "Hi, this is Taylor. I love your song, but I need you to change one line."

"Which one?"
"The one about the saxophone."

I loved that line. Had that object writing thing going . . . *lonely saxophone.*

"Can I ask why?"
"'Cause I ain't got a f***ing saxophone in my band."
"OK."
"Call you back in five minutes."

When she did, I had a couple of brand-new saxless lines for her to choose from. She picked one and hung up. She was true to her word, did a great version, and sold gold. It wouldn't be the last time an artist asked to change a lyric.

One last note on your lyric: if your intent is to pitch your song, give some thought to who would record it. If your lyric paints an unflattering picture of the narrator, is there an artist willing to be seen in that light? Does the story line require the artist to be older, have a family? Your lyric choices can narrow the possibilities for pitching sometimes.

So you've gathered more tools. How's your lyric looking?

**"**

**If you have one mantra as a lyricist, let it be "Show. Don't tell."**

**"**

# CHAPTER 4

# YOUR LYRIC'S LOOKING GOOD!

**Hanging with Paul Carrack, Chorleywood, England.**

You've been writing your lyric, and it's looking pretty good on the page, if you do say so yourself.

Now's a good time to remember that lyrics are only half of the song. Doesn't matter if it reads like Shakespeare or if it sings even better than it reads. Talk it out loud. Don't sing it, don't read it in your head, talk it out loud. Section by section, verse by verse, chorus by . . . you get the point. Say the words aloud. Say them until you feel like they would really come out of your mouth. Just like conversation. Write like you talk.

One of the most common tools I use in coaching lyricists is to ask them to put the lyric aside and just tell me what it's about. I take notes and, I swear, every time there are lines that are spoken, they are ten times better than the written ones. Put those in the lyric. That simple.

Maybe the most useful advice I got regarding working on lyrics was to talk them out again once you've committed them to paper. Take a section at a time and just talk it out . . . endlessly. Does your second verse sound like your first verse as far as the cadence and rhythm of the lyric? Does the language seem the same, is it in character, and again, does it sound conversational? Are your rhyme schemes consistent? Are you writing like you talk?

Rhyme schemes are tricky buggers. For instance, you've created a template for your verses in the first verse, but you find the third verse has a brand-new one, totally different than that first one. You might be bored or just being creative, but for me, it's usually a case of simply losing track. Talking them out loud can bring you back to earth. Rhyme schemes are one of the ways a listener learns your song, so throwing them a curve later in the lyric is downright unfair.

**One more reason** I love to talk a lyric out is because I've written with some great singers. I'm not just talking about the ones who have recorded my songs but also the ones who've been in the same room, cocreating.

Paul Carrack comes to mind.

Paul has one of the coolest voices on the planet—you can hear him on "The Living Years," "How Long," and one of my top five songs I wish I'd written, "Tempted." When you throw out a lyric, and someone like Paul sings it back to you, you just want to move on because it sounds so good.

Brenda Russell and I had the pleasure of writing two songs with Paul for his *Blue Views* solo record. Brenda and I were writing as a team in the Ma Maison Hotel in LA years ago. Paul walked into the session just as we were throwing out some ideas for a song that became "Always Have, Always Will." As soon as he started singing, we turned into fans or maybe fan stenographers or maybe fanographers, whatever—anything and everything sounded great. We had to check ourselves and go back through the lyric to make sure it stood the talk test. I've had the same experience with Wynonna Judd, Peter Cox, Cher, and many more. It's easy to get fooled by singing or reading a lyric. Talking it out is the first line of defense.

Another good technique is to find a way to say or write a word without actually using the word. Takes practice and imagination, but you can master it. The sun could be a bright, burning ball, the moon a faint, midnight lover. Don't immediately settle for what your eye sees to describe something. Let your mind wander.

I preach the idea of making lists to every writer I coach. I know it's been written about in recent years in different ways. Pat Pattison talks about finding the "key of your lyric." I was first introduced to a similar idea in Nashville in the early days of coming to co-write. A writer I was working with reached a point in the lyric process that talked about a woman's hair. He stopped, grabbed a thesaurus (I know, that sounds old-school, but one of those, along with Clement Wood's *The Complete Rhyming Dictionary* and William Zinsser's *On Writing Well*, should be required reading for a songwriter), and started to make a list. A list of women's hair colors. He spent a fair amount of time before returning to the lyric, and now, instead of red, he started to pull words such as *fire, auburn,* and *flame* into the lyric. Great stuff. Also, it's a good idea to sprinkle your lyric with words in the family of the main word of your title. For example, if you're writing a lyric with the word *broken* in your title, you are going to be looking for words that relate to "broken." *Shattered, cracked,* even *Humpty Dumpty* . . . get as imaginative as possible here.

I write lyrics as well as music and have been called into writing situations where I have to be responsible for one or the other. One of the first things I try to figure out is the role of the lyric, if that's my job. The best way I ever heard this explained was, "Is your song meant to move the butt or the brain?" Big difference. If your song is for an introspective singer-songwriter, you're going to pay extra attention to the words. If you're Daft Punk, be a slave to the rhythm. It's all good.

**Think of your song** as two elements that have to coexist in the same space. Sounds simple, but it's something I never thought about until I came to Nashville. You've heard the phrase, "Three chords and the truth." The idea is, if you're writing a lyric-driven song, you're good keeping the music part dead simple. Keep the focus on the story. The opposite is also true. If your melody is killer, and you complicate it with a ton of words, it's only going to make your song a hot mess. Serve the song and you can't go wrong.

I'm big on tools and one of my favorites is to cut and paste your lyric. Why? By the time you've written that third verse, you usually have a better handle of what you're writing about. Try taking that verse and moving it up to the first verse slot. The tough part is, now you've raised the bar. This might also work to hook the listener by not telling your story in the conventional, chronological way. Start from the end, tell it backward, begin in the middle, mix it up. Trust that the listener will make the trip with you if it's interesting.

One of the most unusual tools in my box came courtesy of my wife, Kathy. I'm always looking for unique names and places, and one day she suggested scanning the obituary section of our local newspaper. It's one of my go-tos when I'm searching for a unique name for a character in a lyric. This is especially useful if you look for someone who's had a very long life. More often than not, their name will be a name you don't hear very often today. One of my clients even wrote a song based on this exercise called "My Life in Ink," using names, places, and details she found in the obituary section of her local paper.

A technique I borrowed from the business world is called Mind Mapping. Take a large whiteboard or a big Post-it note, write your title in the middle, and circle it. I would suggest placing this board or note somewhere other than where you usually write. Maybe the kitchen or hallway. Someplace you walk by often. When you do, just glance at the word in the middle and if it suggests something, add it to the board with an arrow pointing toward the title you've circled. It's one more way to get your subconscious involved. Once you've filled all the space around your title, take the board or note into the place you write and see what you have.

Like everything else in songwriting, there's no one way. John Lennon is one of my heroes, and he could be at times raw and painfully real and other times a psychedelic Lewis Carroll. Hal David wrote the lyrics to most of Burt Bacharach's classic songs. His lyrics were never fussy and served the song. I got asked to write a lyric for a Burt Bacharach melody co-written with my friend Eliot Kennedy. I was in Sheffield, England, at the time, and it was probably good that I didn't have time to think about it. I walked around Sheffield and thought about the type of lyric Hal David might have written. The song was called "If You Can Find It in Your Heart," and I hope I did it justice. I heard Burt loved it. That was enough for me. We also heard Luther Vandross loved it and had planned on recording it. Sadly, he passed way too soon. I would have loved to have heard that incredible voice on our song.

Why am I suddenly going on about Burt Bacharach? Because, for my money, he has written some of the most amazing melodies of the past hundred years. Next stop on our journey? Melody.

**"**

**Is your song meant to move the butt or the brain?**

**"**

# CHAPTER 5

# WRITING A KILLER MELODY

**Killer writing day with my buddy Eliot Kennedy.**

Do you know how the average listener learns your song? Chorus melody. That guy or girl in the car wants to hear something they can sing. Not the whole song, not your well-crafted lyric, not your infectious track . . . they need to be able to sing something—now!

Once they have the chorus melody in their head, it's about the title. Think of it this way. You call your best friend and say, "Hey, I just heard the coolest song." He says, "Yeah? Sing it to me." You sing a bit of the melody, and then he asks the title of the song so he can learn it, too. If he gets it, he may focus on what it's actually saying in the chorus. If he digs deeper, he goes for the verses and the other parts. It's all about the chorus—in this case, the chorus melody. Most listeners will never get past the singing-the-chorus stage. You want to make it one of those ear worms, a "can't get it out of my head" melody.

**There's a famous story** in songwriting circles of the hit writer Albert Hammond riding down an elevator when one of his songs comes on. There's only one other person in the elevator with him, and as they descend, Albert can't contain himself any longer and says, "Hear that song? I wrote that lyric!" Without missing a beat, the other passenger says, "You can't whistle a lyric," and leaves it at that.

Doesn't matter if you write music first, lyrics first, or write to tracks, no matter. The melody is still king.

There are countless books on theory and rules to follow to help you understand melody construction, but I got nothing here. A little background is in order.

I went to Berklee College of Music in Boston the first time they decided to let in the rock 'n' roll kids. This was the summer of 1970. Looking back, I'm sure it was adapt or die for the school, and money talks, so . . . I could barely read music but passed the audition as a bass player. I was also writing songs (badly) but couldn't begin to translate them to notation. I was intimidated.

Day one, 8:00 a.m., I headed to my very first teacher meeting. As I opened the door, I was met with a huge cloud of sweet-smelling tobacco. When the smoke cleared, sitting there was Major "Mule" Holly. This guy had played bass with everyone from Charlie Parker and Ella Fitzgerald to Frank Sinatra, Duke Ellington, and Quincy Jones. I figured I was going to be outed right there. Found out, busted, and sent home.

Instead, he asked me to just "play."

"I can barely read," I said.

"You can learn that; you can't learn to 'play.'"

I played, he liked me, I lived another day. I went away understanding I might not know the rules, but I could create. I could play.

Every writer should try and get as much information as possible. I wish I'd stayed at Berklee longer than the one semester I attended and learned all I could for my path. John Mayer had a similar stay at Berklee. I urge you to search YouTube for his talks with students. Fantastic stuff. The takeaway for me was, gather as much information as you can, but if you can't turn it into inspiration, it can lose its value.

I'm a judge at Belmont University in Nashville for their "Commercial Music Showcase" once a year. I envy those young artists and songwriters getting the best of both worlds, surrounded by pros and able to apprentice on Music Row. Get it while you can. You need all the tools you can get on this journey. Even if school isn't your path, learn a few of the tools that will produce dividends for your songwriting pretty quick. For example:

- The circle of fifths is a must.
- The Nashville number system is a smart alternative to full-on notation.

- I still love picking up a Beatle's songbook and playing along using the chord diagrams. I always come away with something new that I'll eventually use.

So I'm not the theory guy, but let's play.

One of my favorite tools for melody is to create away from the guitar, my main instrument. I might sit in my studio and play keyboards, might start with a drum loop to get in a groove and go from there to laying down a chord change. I'll start singing something over the changes, and it may even feel pretty good. I'll record it just in case, but what I really love to do is record those chord changes and get away from my studio. I know the act of creating a melody might come from doing it while you're playing, but for me, singing it over the changes I've recorded away from an instrument gives me more freedom to experiment with my melody. Anytime you can create an environment of freedom with your melody, instead of being part of a performance, can only be great.

Just starting your melody from some note other than the root of your chord can create a more interesting melody. If the root note of your chord is a C and you sing a seventh over that to start, you've already created some tension and made the melody more interesting.

**A tried-and-true** method to creating interesting melodies is to pick up an unfamiliar instrument. In short, don't be afraid to suck. Play like a kid and see where it takes you. If you get out of your comfort zone, you can't rely on your usual tricks, and you just might find some melodic magic.

Deconstructing melodies is a good shortcut to making your own great ones. Take a current song and spend some time making notes. Where does the melody start out? What's the highest note? Is there tension and release in the melody? Where does it show up? I've even picked a melody out on guitar and visualized it as a box or a graph. Where is the lowest note in the melody? Where is the highest? How do the notes in between relate to those highs and lows? Visualizing the melody is a good tool that doesn't require a theory background.

I talked about cutting and pasting in the lyric section, but it's just as important here. Once you have a melody in mind for the verse and chorus, try flipping them. Is your chorus melody really a stronger verse melody? Is your bridge melody a cool chorus melody? Might be worth a cut-and-paste just to see.

At the end of the day, make sure you can't get the melody out of your head. Can you sing it in the car, on a walk? My favorite test is if someone who has been in the general vicinity while you're creating it starts singing it. Second best is when you play it for someone and later on you hear them humming it.

I coach quite a few lyricists and not all have a knack for melody. I get them to write a lyric to an existing, familiar melody. It can give structure for them so that at the end of the day they have a lyric. Inspired by an existing song but not connected to it. With apologies to John Lennon and Elton John, "whatever gets you through the write."

So how can you come away with something fresh, interesting, and impossible for someone to get out of their head? I'll pick my top five to focus on.

1. **Rhythm**

   Nothing gets more boring than hearing the same melodic rhythm throughout the whole song. There are some things you can try, from doubling up the number of notes in the chorus to trying the opposite. Short notes in the verse, long notes in the chorus, halftime in the bridge, stops, builds, anything to mix it up.

2. **Length of Phrase**

   Similar to the rhythm fixes in that you want to mix it up. If every melodic section has the same number of lines and words per line, it's going to get old quick. Try tapping out the words and make sure your sections are not all the same.

3. **Range**

   Another place your melody can bog down is the range, or lack of range. One of the reasons we respond to some songs and singers is the emotion they put into the melody. If your melody is rooted in one area throughout, it's hard to get it to take off. There are a million hits that feature the same chord changes from verse to chorus with the chorus being an octave up. Instant drama. Range can also serve to create moments in your melody. Think of singers such as Whitney Houston, Aretha Franklin, and those times the melody takes you to new heights in the song.

4. **Your Comfort Zone**

   Learn to leave it. For me, this means trying different instruments, different tunings, but most importantly, listening to music that's different than what I'm working on. For instance, if you write rock, listen to classical, jazz, country, opera . . . You'll be surprised by how much will creep into your melodies. I'm not talking about sitting down and dissecting every style of music. Just let it seep

in. You are your influences. The wider your influences, the
more chances of blending them into something unique.

5. **Subconscious**
Don't sit down and say, "This melody fits here because
of the chord change," or "This is just how I do it." Take
some time to let that subconscious in. That's where it can
go from being "nice" to being magical. It's also one of the
ways your voice as a writer comes in. One simple trick:
record your melody at any stage and just let it loop. At
home, in the car, running errands. Just give it time to be
the best it can be.

In early 2000, I signed as a writer with Steelworks-Universal in
Sheffield, England. I had been writing with Eliot Kennedy, and
Steelworks was his baby. Eliot is one of the most inspirational,
amazing, multitalented people on the planet.

Eliot pulled me in to write with many of the artists coming
through Steelworks' doors. The Spice Girls (David Beckham hung
out in the kitchen most days—great guy), 5, Ronan Keating, and
many more. They came to write, do pre-production, and finally,
to the main studio to record their albums. It was very much like
a modern-day Motown.

In early 2000, I wasn't in Sheffield but at my home in Franklin,
Tennessee when I got an email from Eliot. He was in the studio
with Billie Piper, a UK superstar in the mold of our Britney Spears.
They had cut much of the album but were in search of a first
single. He asked if I had anything. This is where most writers, me
included, usually lie, say yes, and go into panic-mode writing. He
said it just had to be a start, with an up-tempo dance beat, and
something different.

I got busy, starting with loops. I had been listening to all kinds of different music at the time, including Middle Eastern melodies. (A great trick passed on to me by Miles Copeland, who had been my publisher a few years earlier. He also managed the Police and Sting, and mentioned Sting would immerse himself in different musical cultures and assimilate them into his own music to stay fresh and inspired. "Desert Rose" comes to mind.)

**I was getting nothing** as the day went on. I kept a loop that I liked going to make sure I stayed up-tempo, but by the end of the morning, I'm just getting loopy and . . . stressed. I knew I had to get away from my studio and do something that involved my left brain. So my wife, Kathy, sent me off to the grocery store with a list.

As I was getting out of the car, I was humming something, walked into the store, still humming whatever it was. Walking down the vegetable aisle, I stopped. At first, I thought it was a melody I had just heard. It was pretty fully formed but had a little bit of a Middle Eastern vibe. I stood there until it dawned on me that I might have made it up. Maybe. I called my home phone and left it on the answering machine. (The iPhone wouldn't be invented for another seven years, so it was all I could do to get it down before it disappeared into the ether for some other songwriter to find.)

I got home as fast as I could, singing this melody nonstop. I recorded it over the loop, listened a few times, and emailed it to Eliot in Sheffield. He was in the studio with his production team of Mike Lever and Tim Percy along with the artist, Billie Piper. Together, they took my melody and ran with it. They finished the song that same night and recorded it the next day. The song was called "Day and Night." It became the first single on the album, entered the UK charts at number one, and sold over 400,000 singles.

If you know the song, my melody is the part underneath this lyric:

> 'Cause the only time I think of you
> Is every day and all night through
> Whenever I breathe you're on my mind
> Every day and night, babe

Still one of the biggest thrills of my life—and a killer melody day.

**Play like a kid and see
where it takes you.**

# CHAPTER 6

# SONG STRUCTURE

**Deconstructing hits.**

The best, simplest way I've heard song structure explained is that the info, the story, and the details are in the verses. The pre-chorus is where the tension happens and makes you want to hear the chorus. The chorus is the BIG FAT IDEA. The bridge is the scenic route on the journey, and the post-chorus reminds you of the BIG FAT IDEA without actually restating all of the BIG FAT IDEA.

**There are so many** ways to structure a song, but staying current is a good place to start writing hits. Listeners' tastes change, and song structure usually reflects the changes. In 1967, the Doors were just one of many bands stretching the limits of radio with seven-minute songs. These days, you're more likely to find them in the three- to three-and-a-half-minute range, sometimes without any of the old building blocks such as bridges and pre-choruses.

I mentioned earlier the difference in writing a song to move the brain or the butt; that choice is always going to influence a song's structure. Deconstruct the type of songs that move you, just for the structure.

If you think of the parts of your song in terms of A, B, and C, it's easy to track: A is your verse, B the chorus, and C the bridge. There are more parts to consider such as the intro, pre-chorus, and post-chorus, but for now, use these three as your standard. Common forms are:

A, A, B, A, B, C, B, B
A, B, A, B, C, B, B

You don't see many A-only songs today (think "I Walk the Line"). Early folk and country utilized this structure, but it's disappeared from radio over time as listeners look for multiple hooks.

Start with the basic forms, but mix and match. Does your song need a bridge? Would it work to start with the chorus or a part of it? Better with pre-choruses or post-choruses? A good guide is to take notes on the song structures you're hearing on the radio now. In coaching songwriters, I tend to see quite a few A, A, B, A, A, B, C, B, B; four verses. I generally ask them to give some thought to paring this down to three whenever possible. Songs in most modern music are shorter these days, and it's always been a matter of "Don't bore us; get to the chorus."

Check the running time of your song before you sign off on it.

This can help you decide what needs to go if you find yourself looking at four-minute songs or more. It's important to think of the listener in this case. You might want to use more repetition and less new information.

Take notes on how the song is constructed. Next time you sit down to write, consider the song you tore apart when you build your own. If you haven't noticed by now, I'm a pretty big fan of deconstruction when it comes to songwriting. It's an eye-opening shortcut to see how the big boys build. When I was starting out, deconstruction meant endlessly dropping the needle down on my favorite records and learning them on guitar—part by part, writing the lyric out by hand. There are easier ways to accomplish this today, but the idea is the same. Keep doing this, and what you learn gets in your songwriter DNA. You get better quick.

Dave Grohl of the Foo Fighters told an interviewer that he writes a bunch of choruses and picks the best one to actually be the chorus. This way, he knows all the other ones will be hooks as well. Great, if you can do it. Bryan Adams once told me he starts with the chorus. He felt if you don't have a hit chorus, you don't have a hit—period. I do like this as a tool to use. Nail the chorus and fill in the structure around it.

Another structure that almost feels like cheating when it works is to start your song with the chorus or a portion of it. If you can hook a listener that fast, the chances of their channel surfing in the car go way down.

When I'm structuring a song, I try to think about moments. We've all heard moments in the performance of a song. Think of singers with big voices; Whitney Houston, Adele, and Celine Dion come to mind. They can bring out the raw emotion in a song, but you can be thinking about those moments as you create yours. What are the real moments, the emotional highs and lows in my song? How do I want to feature them when I'm putting the song together? You can create a moment with a modulation. Tread carefully here; you can also create a cringe-worthy moment that you can't get back. Space (silence in your arrangement) can be built into the structure and doesn't have to rely only on the singer.

Try to let the song dictate the structure rather than any rules you come across. You're looking for happy accidents, and mixing up the structure might provide one once in a while. The Beatles' "A Day in the Life" was created by crashing two different song ideas together. Lennon had the trippy part but was stuck on finishing when McCartney played him an unfinished song of his own. The "woke up, got out of bed" section was a perfect counterpoint to what Lennon had written. When I first read that story, the technique went directly into my toolbox.

Daniel Levitin, an American neuroscientist described what Lennon and McCartney achieved really well in his book *This Is Your Brain on Music*:

> **Music is organized sound, but the organization has to involve some element of the unexpected or it's emotionally flat and robotic. The artist artfully manipulates our expectations with a semi-resolution that straddles surprise and release.**

Yeah, what he said.

**You also know** by now that I'm not a rules guy, but the challenges of creating song structure can make a strong case for the saying, "Learn the rules first so you can break them later."

So your music and lyric are looking good. Next stop . . .

**"**

**Try to let the song dictate the structure rather than any rules you come across.**

**"**

CHAPTER 7

# IS YOUR SONG DONE?

**All smiles after finishing our song "Don't You Talk
to Me like That" with Vinx and Brenda Russell.**

I coach songwriters to slow down. When I hear "I wrote this in
ten minutes," I'm scared. You might have had ten minutes of inspiration but zero minutes of editing. One of the big differences
between the amateur songwriter and the pro? Rewriting. It's hard.
That's why so many novice writers don't do it. "The fun is in the
inspiration, not the perspiration." I hear you, but there are no
points for fast.

**Nobody cares** how long it took Allen Shamblin and Mike Reid to
write the Bonnie Raitt classic "I Can't Make You Love Me." They

only care that it's one of the most awesome songs of all time. Most of the pro writers I know and work with are master craftsmen. They take their time. There's an old saying about writing: "You write your first draft with your heart . . . You rewrite with your head." Use your head.

Here are a few things I might ask myself before signing off on a song:

- Is it relatable? Am I writing about something that people will really care about?
- Am I showing or just telling? This is a biggie, especially here in Nashville. Have I included enough color and detail to make a listener see what I want them to see?
- Is there a better concept out there? Is there a better, more unique way to tell my story?
- Does my song breathe? Is there plenty of space for the lyric and the melody to coexist, or is it a challenge for a listener?
- Is my chorus memorable? Can you go away humming it?
- Have I been self-indulgent? Just because it's in my own head doesn't mean it has to be in the final version.
- Is the intro a hook or just a space to fill?
- Is my bridge a real departure from everything else? Do I even need a bridge?
- Is EVERYTHING in my song a hook?
- Is there too much information in my song? Info belongs in the verses and bridge, but if the story continues long into the chorus, it's a great way to lose a listener.
- How long is my song? This is where I have to be realistic.
- Check the idea. How interesting is it? Will the title work to pull someone in?
- Have I referenced back to my prose to make sure I have supported the title/idea?

- On the melody side, does my chorus lift?
- Have I studied current song structure?
- Do I LOVE IT?

If you play live, you can use your audience as a focus group for your song. These are the people who hopefully would be buying what you're selling. If you don't play live and don't have the option of a publisher yet, give your lyric to a friend, ask them to go away and come back and tell you what your lyric is about. If they can't, you have to ask yourself if you've written it clearly or if the idea is more in your head than on the page.

**Before I make up my mind** on a lyric, I might try it from another perspective. Is it better written in second or third person? I don't know, but I might try. Have I compromised anywhere in my song? Made the right choices? Does it move me? Believe me, the best ones will move you first, and if they do, the odds of the song moving someone else are great.

Psychologist Scott Barry Kaufman is credited with coming up with the four stages of creativity, which John Braheny mentions in his book *The Craft and Business of Songwriting* as well. When I'm coaching, this is how I explain them:

1. **Preparation.** This is the subject of chapter 2 ("What's the Big Idea?"), in which you intentionally look for things to write about: lines, titles, making your list. You're preparing to write. Maybe not today, but in the future.
2. **Incubation.** Let these ideas, lines, and titles marinate.
3. **Illumination.** Remember the stuff about the good stuff? The real details? This is where you put it. Begin to shed light on this idea you found. Start with real things. From your mind's eye to the page.

4. **Verification.** Finally. Here's where you bring the editor back to life and put him to work.

So how do these four stages work?

First, if I can say I looked for the best idea possible for my song, let it sit awhile rather than settling on the first thing that came to mind, started writing my lyric with the real stuff and did not just begin by making my lyric look good (clever words and rhymes) on paper, and left the editor/critic out all along the way until step 4, I'm good. I don't necessarily think about these stages while I'm writing but wait until I'm happy with my song and then double-check these stages to make me that much more confident that I've written the best song I can.

Done is fun. There's nothing better than when you've finished a great song, having reached the point where you sit back and feel like you've performed a magic trick—pulled something out of thin air. It's great to be a songwriter at that moment.

My song is done. Now what?

**Done is fun. There's nothing better than when you've finished a great song.**

# CHAPTER 8

# TIME TO DEMO

**Mentoring the fabulous Songwriting Academy members at their 2016 Andalusian songwriting retreat in Spain.**

Have a plan for your song.

Here's a step that most beginning songwriters don't put a lot of thought into but need to.

I want to cry when a writer I'm coaching tells me stories about spending $1,500 on a demo or that they used a demo service guaranteed to give your songs that "Nashville sound." I'm not saying spending your hard-earned money on a great demo is a bad idea. What I will say is, make sure the song is killer first. I don't mean nice; I mean great. So much money is pissed away by songwriters without a plan. We all love our babies, but not all of them need to go to Ivy League schools. Some are community college songs, some are vocational school songs, and some are minimum wage songs. Think hard and be objective. Is your song worth spending money on? Does it deserve to go beyond the home demo stage?

This is where a publisher can be so right even when it feels so wrong. I've sat in meetings where my publisher might tell me my newest baby is good or even great, but then, ask, "Where are we going to pitch it? Do we have a plan? Does it make sense to spend money to have a full-blown version without a plan?" Usually, the answer is no.

You may not have a publisher to tell you any of this. You have to decide. Is the song good if it's stripped down to a guitar or piano vocal version? I'm talking songs, not records. Some hits are great records, but they may not be great songs. There can be a difference sometimes. Monster hits such as "Uptown Funk" are fantastic records with irresistible production, but is it a great song? Lots of current pop hits are built over one constant chord change, with the production element building over them (think Ed Sheeran's "Shape of You"). If you take away the production factor, does it still work as a song?

**You can't polish** a turd, and you cannot disguise a bad song by throwing money at it. Again, how good is the song? Be objective. Have you played it outside of friends and family? Face it, friends and family love you, and they'll love your song. They can't be the reason for spending money in the studio. Hit writers don't demo every idea. Neither should you.

Let's talk about a few common mistakes. I was a mentor at a

retreat in Spain in 2016 when a UK-based writer asked if he could play me a couple of country songs he'd just had demoed by a Nashville demo studio. They sounded fine and were pretty good pitches for Nashville . . . if it was 1990. The idea had been done and done, the demo sounded dated, and the terms he thought of as "country" were stereotypical terms that you just don't hear in country songs anymore. Did he, I asked, listen to current country radio? "Not much, but I like the major artists like Kenny Rogers and Dolly Parton." He was aiming for the '90s or even '80s country market. The result was totally outdated and unable to be pitched.

Do your homework and understand the market before you write the song and spend money on demoing. In other words, have a plan.

Another common mistake some writers make is not doing their research. They write the "perfect Taylor Swift song." They can imagine hearing her sing it, so they demo it. Cold truth, Taylor's not going to do the song. Look at the writer credits; she writes her own songs or writes with a team. She's not looking for songs. It's a shot in total darkness. Write for the up-and-comers or the artists who aren't songwriters.

One more demo kiss of death: DIY demos.

You bought some gear. You want to save money by playing and singing everything. Unless your chops are as good as the late, great Prince, don't submit that version of your song as a demo. You want the song to shine. Don't give a publisher, producer, or artist any reason to be turned off. That reason can be an outdated drum sound, overused keyboard patch, less-than-stellar vocal.

Unless you're trying to get attention as a producer or artist, nobody cares that you can do it all. Even if you can, this isn't the showcase for you. It's all about the song.

Let's say you've taken all this into account and you still decide to demo. Can you get your song across with a simple demo? By simple, I still mean great. I've had songs recorded with just a guitar and vocal, but I was sure to use the best guitarist I know and the best singer for the job. Ballads can work well with this treatment, although ballads are the toughest songs to get cut simply because there are so many being written. If you go this route, consider adding one color instrument to your simple demo. Could be harmonica, cello, banjo, mandolin—anything to add some vibe.

If your song is up-tempo, that's where the price might go up but be a good investment. If you need a real band to get the excitement across, then go for it. I've spent close to $2,000 on a couple of songs in the past, but it was worth the roll of the dice to give that producer or artist something they could just "slip into."

Some writers I coach have given me examples, maybe bootleg recordings of a writer's song getting cut from a pretty raw demo. Those usually boil down to two things. The writer has a long track record and doesn't need to polish his recording, or the song is just that good. I'm a big John Hiatt fan, and I've heard some rough demos with just him and an electric guitar, letting it rip. He checks both boxes and has gotten some great covers, including Bonnie Raitt, Ray Charles, and Bob Dylan.

The powers that be can want very different things. I know publishers who would rather have a bare-bones demo than a demo that sounds like a record. Same with producers and artists. Chris Oglesby, VP of Creative at BMG Nashville, is a songwriter's champion and an old friend. He's a no BS song guy. You write a great song, he'll know it. Not everyone in the industry is like that. Study the people you hope to get your song to. For every Chris, there are dozens of people in the business who need to hear a recorded, full-blown version of a hit before they commit.

**The epiphany** for me came one day in Nashville when I got together with two of my favorite co-writers, Kye Fleming and Brenda Russell to write for a few days. All of us had seen some success, but we also had war stories of getting songs on hold for some of our favorites, only to have them fall through at the eleventh hour. We sat down that first day and said, "Let's just write for ourselves. Forget what a publisher is asking for or what we think an artist will love. Let's just write something *we* love." For the next two days, we just wrote.

We brought elements of each of us into the room without a thought, other than to see if we could get each other excited. We did—to the point of hugs and tears and running to the nearest studio to record our little creation.

Cut to the chase: that song made its way to the very artist we had all been targeting for a few years—Tina Turner, a megastar at the time. This song sounded nothing like anything we had ever heard her do, much less like one of her recent hits. We saw her interviewed on *Oprah* talking about how she found the song to build her next album around and what it meant to her. Wow.

If you hear the demo, it's a drum loop, my simple keyboard part, Bill McDermott (who also recorded the demo for us) on guitar, and Brenda on vocal. It was one of the simplest demos I've ever been a part of. We were only trying to capture the feeling.

That simple demo was the inspiration for Trevor Horn's mega production of our song "Dancing in My Dreams" on the album *Wildest Dreams*, which went on to sell over six million.

That was the little demo that could . . . So can yours? If the answer is yes, let's get it out there!

**So much money is pissed away by songwriters without a plan.**

# PART 2

# THE BUSINESS
## (AND THE PERILS)

4th March 1973

United Artists Records, Inc.
6920 Sunset Boulevard
Los Angeles, California 90028

Gentlemen:

This will acknowledge that simultaneously herewith we have entered into a series
of Agreements ("Agreements") with Terry Knight Enterprises, Ltd., and its sub-
sidiaries, divisions and affiliates ("TKE") which contain various terms and pro-
visions granting TKE certain rights regarding our services both individually and
collectively as a group p/k/a "FAITH".

As a consideration for our entering into said Agreements, TKE has acknowledged
that our services are special, unique and extraordinary and has therefore agreed
that it will not UNDER ANY CIRCUMSTANCES reveal to any third party:

       a)  Our true identities;

       b)  Our legal and/or professional names;

       c)  Our professional background;

       d)  Our citizenship or national origins;

       e)  Any information whatsoever of a personal,
           professional or private nature, without
           our prior written consent.

Very truly yours,

_____
(Lead Guitar/Vocals)

_____
(Drums)

_____
(Bass Guitar/Vocals)

_____
(Keyboards/Vocals)

_____
(Lead Vocals)

TERRY KNIGHT ENTERPRISES, LTD.

By _____
TERRY KNIGHT
President

RECORD WORLD APRIL 7, 1973

**Be careful what you "sign." Terry Knight's plan to hype the band.
No names. Let the music speak for itself. Big-time backlash.**

# CHAPTER 9

# GETTING YOUR SONG "OUT THERE"

You have the song, you have the demo, you know it's great. Now it's time to get someone else to agree. Let's talk about the players and the path to getting your song heard, recorded, released, and . . . making money.

**Publishers.** A publisher is still the holy grail for a songwriter. Their job is to support your efforts to get your song heard as well as to nurture you in the process. This can include an advance to help you have more time to devote to writing, paying for your demos, and being on the lookout for labels, producers, and artists looking for songs for their next record. When they find them, they send your song to them. They also take care of the registration (copyright) and administration (office details) of your song.

What would a publishing deal actually look like in 2019? It would be a lot like courting before marriage. You both have an idea of what you want, but you're taking it slow. A publisher might offer a single song contract. This almost never involves an advance. The publisher may offer to use his or her expertise and best efforts to promote your songs for a limited period, maybe two years.

If, during that time, the song gets recorded and released, they may be able to keep whatever share of publishing they asked for in the contract. Starting out, that's probably 100 percent of the publisher's share. In the event your song doesn't get picked after two years, all rights revert to you. The deal's off.

You may have to prove yourself through a few of these single song deals before the publisher proposes marriage—a long-term deal. This is where you're looking at an advance. An advance means enough to help you devote more time to writing more potential hits. This money is not free. It's recoupable. This means the first income made is given to the publisher until your debt (advance) is paid. This is a big deal. Let's say you're offered a four-year contract. It will be one year guaranteed with three options. These are not your options; they are the publisher's. If at the end of the first year, the publisher panics because you're not generating enough income to repay the advances; the deal may be off. You get the point; you need to make money!

So how do you get a publisher to love you enough to offer you a deal in 2019? You write singles. More than this, you write HIT singles. This is where the performance money comes into the picture. A hit single like Adele's "Someone like You" has generated somewhere in the neighborhood of $900,000 in songwriting royalties. Ideally, you want your song to be a single and make a slow climb up the charts and have a long shelf life. I'm stressing this part based on my own experiences. I co-wrote a massive single in the UK by Billie Piper called "Day and Night." The single entered the charts at number one on May 27, 2000. Fantastic to be sure, but it went back down again just about as fast! Performance income was good but not huge. My publisher was happy because the performance income is split 50/50 between the publisher and the songwriter.

You might ask, "Why do I have to worry about singles? How about just getting my song on an album?" I hear you. A little history here to help you see the reason why:

I love Apple. As a creative, I've bought and used every Apple product to hit the market. I love innovation and technology. But when iTunes was introduced, every songwriter I know had to take a deep breath. Now you could cherry-pick from an album only the songs you really wanted to have. I'm talking prestreaming here. If my song is on an album, even one by a major artist, my song might not be the one you bought. For that freedom of choice, I don't get paid. Simple as that. If I don't get paid, neither does my publisher. If the publisher doesn't get paid often enough, he can't offer the advances that he used to for his signed writers, much less the aspiring ones. The pie has now officially shrunk. The income from mechanicals (money made from physical product) really takes a nosedive, and the songwriter, like me, who made a good living from album cuts is now cut out. Ironic that the very progress I loved didn't love me back here, no? At least my iPod was letting me take all my favorite songs on vacation. iTunes was released on January 9, 2001. My birthday.

On the subject of money, let's talk about the ways you can make it through your songwriting. There are three main sources of income. Performance royalty, mechanical royalty, and sync fees.

**Performance Royalty.** This is the money a songwriter gets when their song is played on the radio, TV, an online streaming service, or performance venue. In the United States, these royalties are collected and paid through a Performing Rights Organization (PRO).

**PROs.** In the United States, it's ASCAP, BMI, or SESAC. PROs collect the performance money and divide it equally between the songwriter and the publisher of the song. If a dollar is earned, the PRO collects it and distributes fifty cents to the songwriter and fifty cents to the publisher.

You might be aware of what PROs do, but do you use them? Do you call up and ask to meet with someone in writer relations? If not, do it. You need a champion in the beginning, and they just might be the one to love what you do and spread the word. They can do it. They don't just collect money for you; they're competitive and always on the lookout for the next Julia Michaels. Makes them look good. These folks collect and distribute overseas income as well. I've had quite a few songs recorded by artists outside the United States, such as Rouge from Brazil who sold over a million and spent ten weeks at number one, and even one of the first Pop Idol winners from the UK, hear'say. Income from your songs might take a little longer to get to you from foreign territories if you're in the United States, but have no fear, it will show up.

**Mechanical Royalty.** These are different than performance royalties. This is the income from paid downloads and physical product such as CDs. The current rate is 9.1 cents per song per download or sale and that's split between the songwriter and publisher. Your PRO does not collect this money. It's paid by whoever has the license to distribute your song on a record or download. Your song will need to be registered with a company that collects mechanical royalties, such as the Harry Fox Agency in the United States, to receive this income. If you self-publish, it's important that you register yourself with an agency like Harry Fox.

**Sync (Synchronization) Fees.** This is income from licensing your song for a movie, TV show, commercial, video game, or anywhere the song is synced with a visual. This sync fee is negotiated and is usually split 50 percent to the songwriters and 50 percent to the artist and record label.

You can be on the lookout for sync opportunities for your song. Having a publisher to do this for you is great, but you can learn to look for small projects to submit your song for, and if it's chosen, you get the check. Keep in mind, in this scenario, your song has to be as good as a record because whoever buys the right to use it is paying for the recording of your song. They will not go to the expense of rerecording it. The good news? Songs used on TV might fetch $3,000. A movie? More like $10,000, and if your song lands in a major commercial, you could be looking at anywhere from $20,000 to half a million. Great money, but you may have more luck starting out finding a low-budget project, because they're more likely to use your song that sounds like Tom Petty than that big hit of Tom's. Much, much cheaper to license for them.

## DO I NEED TO COPYRIGHT MY SONGS?

I mentioned a publisher can register your song, and protecting your song is important. However, keep in mind, in this day and age, your work is protected just by getting it out there for people to hear. You can post your songs on Soundcloud, on your cell phone, in songwriting groups—all proofs of creation. At some point, you will want to register it with the United States Copyright Office, but wait until you're sure you're not going to make any changes because you pay each time to register the work. My publishers never registered a song until it was to be released on a record.

**Copyright Types.** Every individual song is made up of two separate copyrights: Composition and Sound Recording (or the master). Composition includes the lyric and the melody, and sound recording means the audio recording. Composition copyright is split between the songwriters and publishers, while the sound recording copyright is split between artists and the record label.

**Streaming.** Some can argue that streaming has resuscitated the music business. But in fact, only the major artists in the world are raking it in. For example, Taylor Swift's song "Shake It Off" earned somewhere between $280,000 and $390,000 for 46.3 million streams. Here are the payout figures on a few of the major streaming services:

| | |
|---|---|
| **Apple Music** | $0.0064 |
| **Spotify** | $0.0038 |
| **Pandora** | $0.0011 |
| **YouTube** | $0.0006 |

We've been talking about fees, splits, and contracts, and one of your biggest advocates could be this next player.

**Entertainment Lawyer.** An entertainment lawyer can play a huge part in promoting you in the music community, but the first step is to make sure you use one to protect your interests when dealing with contracts.

Some of the best breaks I've had have come from entertainment lawyers who have hooked me up with other music business clients of theirs. Again, makes them look good, and you benefit from the connections.

It worked for me. In 1983, I was living in Los Angeles, having quit my Hoosier-based band, Faith, which by now was on a downward spiral (although its members were still making a good living playing clubs). Me? I was working the only day job I've ever had to this day (thank you, God), at Bullock's department store in Sherman Oaks. My friend Bill Wray had just gotten a record deal, liked my writing, and recorded a couple of my songs. He introduced me to his lawyer, John Frankenheimer, of Loeb and Loeb. John was a heavy hitter in the LA music scene and, to this day, is a huge name in entertainment law.

**I couldn't afford** to park near the Century City offices of Loeb and Loeb, much less pay the lawyer's hourly fee. Bill took me in to meet with John. John listened to what I had been writing and agreed to represent me on the spot. He said something to the effect of "Don't worry about paying me now. Let's see what we can get going for the future." He got me in front of Diana Ross and she recorded the first cover I ever had, called "Shock Waves," with legendary producer Tom Dowd. I stayed with Loeb and Loeb through an artist deal and three publishing deals. I hope I rewarded the faith John had in me. He was an early champion of mine, and I'm eternally grateful.

How do you get in front of *your* John Frankenheimer? You may have to pay for that first appointment just to be able to show what you can do, but if they love your songs, they can open doors you haven't dreamed of.

The conventional routes, such as just dropping off a package at a publisher or record label's door or, worse yet, mailing your song, just don't exist these days. For one thing, it's way too time consuming for them to listen to everything. Let's be honest, if there were no gatekeepers, every publisher, label person, and producer's desk would resemble Mount Everest. They would be overwhelmed. If your song came through known channels such as an industry person, entertainment lawyer, or anyone doing business regularly with the powers that be, that will at least give you the chance of getting heard.

Probably the biggest reason you need help in getting your songs to the right people is plagiarism or fear of plagiarism. A case in point:

Miles Copeland was managing Sting as well as running his publishing company, Bugle Songs, in the early '80s when he received notice that he was being sued, or rather Sting was being sued, by a songwriter who had sent his songs, unsolicited, to Bugle. This writer claims someone there must have listened to his submission because he had not only written the mega hit "Every Breath You Take," but the whole *Synchronicity* album! He claimed the whole album—no lie. As insane as this idea was, it still took some lawyering up and money on Miles's part to make it go away. Dealing with an unsolicited submission is just too risky.

So find a champion wherever you can and get as much traction as possible to make the case for your songwriting. Let's say you've followed all the steps so far and utilized the resources I've mentioned, and you get a bite. A publisher offers to do their thing, which means they get your song in front of an artist.

This is a good time to remind you about lawyers. Have that contract looked over by one before you sign it. It's exciting to get an offer, but I can tell you from sad personal experience, it might not be a good deal. For instance, if you're an artist and you're upset with the lack of attention from your record label, you would normally have someone else on your team talk to the label head to try and figure it out. If your label head is also your manager, you have zero leverage. Same with having your publisher wear two hats. Not happy with your publishing deal? Your manager is also your publisher? When you have a problem, who ya gonna call? This is what happened to me on two occasions. First with Terry Knight, who wore all three hats—publisher, manager, and label head—and that one took years to sort out. This was one very big misstep for me. He was the superstar manager of Grand Funk Railroad, and we were his next big act to break. All I saw was the massive hype he was able to generate about the band's first album and trusted it would all go according to his master plan. The plan blew up, leaving myself and the band enslaved to a terrible three-headed monster of a deal leading to years of legal wrangling. Here's the second bad decision:

Around 1984, I formed a band called Moviola to showcase my songs. I wanted to play live to get songs out there, but I was still on the artist path as well in LA. I had all the affirmation I needed after Virgin Music had given me a small publishing deal for four of my songs. The band was made up of my friend from Faith Band, Carl Storie, my old friends, Bob Terry and Dave Kelly, and a guitarist from Louisville named Hank Linderman.

So now the band was playing wherever we could to support ourselves and playing as many of my songs as we could get away with in between Huey Lewis and Phil Collins covers. One night, we were at Beach Bum Burt's in Redondo Beach. I noticed the same guy had been standing at the bar listening for a few nights in a row. Finally, he came up and introduced himself to Carl and me: Bob

Davis, former executive at MCA Records, entertainment lawyer, and instrumental in the careers of some major artists, including John Mellencamp.

Bob was interested in the band, and we started meeting with him over the next month. The band had been on the verge of breaking up, so this presented a problem. Bob sent a demo we had done with a few of my songs to Billy Gaff, the former manager of Rod Stewart and John Mellencamp, in London. Billy also had a record label called Riva Records. Billy loved what he heard, especially a song of mine called "Heaven Only Knows."

We were in . . . with one small problem: the fractured band. We told Bob, Bob told Billy, Billy said, "I really want only the singer and the songwriter anyway." The band split. Carl (the singer) and I packed up, moved to London, and signed a record/management/ publishing deal with Billy Gaff's company.

Here's the cautionary part. Never, never, ever put all your eggs in one basket. Because if that basket starts to unravel, you're talking to the same customer service guy. Carl and I had made the same mistake the first go-round with Terry Knight by trusting him to wear too many hats as the label head, publisher, and manager. We did it again with Billy Gaff. Who cared? We were going to be huge, and we liked Billy.

**Up until we didn't**. Billy had personal problems and business problems, including feuding with the parent company, Warner, in the United States. The album we had recorded in London with an A-list of session guys was dead in the water. I should have seen the writing, literally on the wall, when I got off the Tube in Central London and saw a huge poster of the album cover with

Carl and me, now called "Blinding Tears," looking like the next big thing. Across the poster someone had written, "Just a couple of Wham! boys!"

Songwriting was again looking like the safer path—except for one big Wham!-sized hitch. Billy owned the publishing rights but didn't have the traditional publishing staff and wasn't about to start hiring song pluggers to get my songs out there. Who ya gonna call? Not my manager—he's part of the three-headed monster who's not paying advances or taking my calls because his artists got dropped after all.

It took me years to get out of that deal and twice as long to get those songs back. Billy also owned the rights to John Mellencamp's classic early songs. Same thing. John was on Riva and managed by Billy. John eventually escaped and tried to buy the rights to his publishing from Billy. When I asked Billy if he sold them back to John, he said, "I never will. Those songs are my retirement."

Your songs may very well be your retirement, but we're nowhere near that point of our journey. Next step . . .

**Find a champion wherever you can and get as much traction as possible.**

## CHAPTER 10

# TAKING THAT BIG MEETING

**Discussing the ins and outs of Nashville with Martin Sutton at the Songwriting Academy's International Songwriting Conference, November 2018, London.**

## OR . . . WHAT YOU HEARD, WHAT THEY MEANT

You've written your song; you've written a GREAT song! You've been getting your song out there, people have heard it, and now you have your first real meeting. The camel's nose is under the tent; you can smell it.

But sometimes that first meeting can . . . well . . . stink.

Sometimes you get the lecture, when all you really want is a yes or a no. A "state of the music business" lesson, when you're really just dying for a little encouragement. An "it's broke," when you want to know how to fix it. Hopefully, you get constructive criticism, but you also might hear some comments or critiques that leave you confused.

## WHAT YOU HEARD, WHAT THEY MEANT

HEARD: "I love this! Not for my artist, but for someone. It's going into my special drawer, the one I go to find that one unique song that fits that artist I'm looking for."

MEANT: They might really mean it as a compliment. It's too good to dismiss but not something they can place. The flip side is, though I've heard this even from my own publishers on occasion, I also know the sheer volume of songs coming in usually makes this a real long shot.

HEARD: "With a few minor fixes, this could be great!" They may suggest some changes, but when you ask if you can send them the edits, they decline.

MEANT: Can be a kiss-off. True, some people (and I've been one of them) do critiques with the best intentions but just don't have time to hear the updates.

HEARD: "Call the next time you're in town."

MEANT: Use your own judgment if you get this response. May be polite or may be a "keep trying but I'm not willing to invest right now" deal.

HEARD: "This would be a great country pitch if Nashville were actually still cutting country songs."

MEANT: Your song is out of step with the current country market.

HEARD: "This one sounds like where the market should be heading; you're a little ahead of the curve right now."

MEANT: Might be a sincere comment, but a smart song person will grab on to potential, so this may fall into the "keep trying" bin.

HEARD: "You're a little behind the curve right now."

MEANT: Your song is outdated.

HEARD: "This is very cool, *but* I already have writers signed to my company whom I can't get cut."

MEANT: Well, this one is often the truth. Think about it. If a publisher is invested in their writer, they don't need outside songs that are very similar in style.

HEARD: "I think you're at that stage where you need to 'write up.'"

MEANT: Usually a compliment but it's easy to go away thinking, "Yeah, of course that would be great, but how?" The publisher is really saying you're writing good songs, ticking most of the boxes, but if you can get with better co-writers, you'll get there quicker.

HEARD: "This might be a hit, but I need a career song."

MEANT: Two ways to take it: (1) "no" or (2) know that the person you're hearing this from really is on a mission to find that "Girl Crush"-esque song.

HEARD: "I *like* it . . . I just don't LOVE it."

MEANT: Man, this one is tough, eh? Been there many times. Your song ticks all the boxes but just doesn't stand out enough to make that person want to run with it. Truth is, your song needs to be unique to stand out from all the others this person has been hearing from established writers. It's hard, but not impossible.

If you hear any of these, don't let them discourage you. Weigh the info and the source, and if you're hearing the same comments over and over, decide how to take them to heart and dig in and, by all means, don't shoot the messenger.

**What do you do?** You fix whatever needs fixing, write some new songs, and go back—and go back soon. Don't be a nuisance, but showing a willingness to take direction is a good thing. Meetings are tricky. I've been in meetings where I had high expectations only to have a publisher stop my song mid-chorus or pick up a call while my song is playing (man, I hate that one). Or they start looking at their email again while my song is playing. They may even stop the meeting to say something like "Good work," or "Thank you for letting me hear your songs." Over and done.

You walk out wondering what just happened. Could be one of a few things: You're not what the publisher is looking for at the moment. You're not quite ready for his full attention. Or he's having a real crap day.

I had a meeting in London years ago with my friend, co-writer, and producer Eliot Kennedy to pitch a Nashville boy band project to Simon Cowell. Yep, that guy. Now, Eliot and Simon were friends and had done business in the past. Simon was looking out the window as we got ushered in, at his new ride, if I remember.

Simon turned around, eventually looked at Eliot, then looked at me and said, "Who are you and why should I care?" I think blood rushed to my head as part of my brain thought he's having the mother of all bad days and hates me already, while the other half of my brain was in a mad scramble to answer the question. Right at that moment, Simon laughed, greeted us properly, and we had a great meeting. You never know what kind of day the person on the other side of the desk is having.

It might just be the start of a relationship for you. It might be the first of many meetings for a publisher to get to know you as a writer and a person. It's pretty rare that that first meeting ends with a handshake and a deal. All those things you've been doing to get your songs heard? Keep on doing them until you get that "yes." Might be a different publisher who finally says that word, but if you're doing great work consistently and keep showing up, someone will get it. Trust me.

**Let's focus on** what it means to "show up." We'll use Nashville as the example. You might get that meeting, and it might go great. Let's say the woman you met with has left the door open. You need to come back soon and often. A town like Nashville is seeing a record number of songwriters moving in; the lady you just met with has countless meetings with promising songwriters. You could very well fall into the "out of sight, out of mind" group if you wait too long in between visits. In order for that publisher to take you seriously, sooner or later you're going to have to physically be in Nashville. I mean move there and be there writing all the time.

There have been a few songwriters who have existed worlds away from Music Row and made it work, but most came here and did the work first. Same for every music center. Sooner or later, when you're ready, I would urge you to make the leap to New York, LA, London, Nashville, or even Atlanta. These are the proving grounds, where the competition is and where the business is. It's where you need to be, hopefully sooner rather than later.

I've made some pretty big leaps of faith when I knew I'd out-grown my opportunities. From my roots in upstate New York to Boston, then to Indiana when the chance came to write for a band with a record deal, then to Los Angeles, to London, and to Nashville more than twenty-three years ago. Some moves were hard, especially in the early years of marriage and raising our girls, but I've never regretted a single minute and never looked back. It's the journey, and the journey sometimes changes course and you have to change with it. I never wanted to be the guy in the Springsteen song who talks about nothing but glory days, or the bitter band guy back home wondering why he never took a chance and bet on his talent. It's a lot like Powerball: "You can't win if you don't play."

Write that song, make that demo, take that meeting, and welcome to the music business.

**Who are you and
why should I care?**

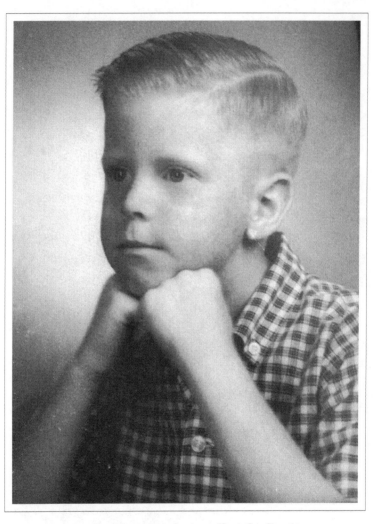

**Pondering some of my earliest feedback,
St. Mary's, Baldwinsville, New York.**

CHAPTER 11

# GETTING FEEDBACK (EVERYBODY'S TALKIN' AT ME)

Pay attention to the charts, common sense, dollars, and cents. Sell out, buy in, can't be taught, it's a gift, it's a curse. I'm better than what's on the radio, radio is dead, labels are obsolete, internet is the shortcut. I wanna be word of mouth, worldwide, boutique, burn bright, burn out, be smart, hip, obscure, Americana. Be a sure bet, long shot, a dark horse. Commercial, confessional, true to myself, and selfless. Work hard but don't let the work show. Honor the new and embrace the old . . . traction and tradition.

Over time, I've heard every one of those words of wisdom.

When it comes to getting your songs out there, my advice? Seek as much wisdom as you can handle. Yep, handle.

When I was a kid, I attended St. Mary's Catholic School in Baldwinsville, New York. We went to confession every Friday in those days, and my buddies and I used to make up a game of confessing exactly the same sins, then comparing the penance we got from the different priests. Always different. Kind of shook our faith in the wisdom of the whole exercise. But we assumed they were experts in their field.

**The advice you get** from different people won't be the same in any field, and music is no different.

Here's a real-life example from one of the singer-songwriters I've coached, Jayne from Dayton, Ohio.

Jayne has made some huge leaps in her writing, especially her lyrics. We focused on this for months, and the change has been fun to watch. All of a sudden, the ideas were more interesting, the mechanics were solid, rhyme schemes, meter, structure . . . better, better, better, and better. She began playing songs for other people, coming to Nashville, attending NSAI (Nashville Songwriters Association International) functions, setting up co-writes and meetings. Here's where the "handle" part comes in.

When I talked to her after a recent Nashville trip, she felt beat up and confused. Some people loved one song but not another. One publisher loved a song but professed to not "know what to do with it." Others suggested lyric changes, music changes, style changes. Listen to what's on the radio, be ahead of the radio, don't pay attention to radio. Listen to every kind of music, focus on current Top 10 Country, write more old school, new school, school's out.

Her problem is not so much with confidence as it is with direction. She got all she could handle, and it didn't always line up. Different strokes for different folks? A publisher I really respect told me, "If you play a song for four people and they all point out the same type of problem with your song, by all means listen and make some changes." Listening is so subjective that you're bound to get some different opinions if you ask enough people. Consider getting opinions of a few people you really respect and who have done the kind of writing you're going for. Research their backgrounds.

I've read critiques from NSAI that have been done by wonderful writers. Even when they differ, they all make some excellent points. Should you make every change they suggest? I urge writers to just try them on. It takes some time to incorporate these new ideas to see if you love them. At the very least, the exercise will give you more tools for your toolbox.

Remember, stay away from spending money on a full-blown demo when getting critiques is your aim. Making these suggested changes after you've blown your budget gets expensive. Gather all the suggestions and *then* head to the studio.

Rules constantly change. It makes sense; we're in a sound-bite society where people take in music in a new way. It's bound to affect how music is made, songs are written, and what's expected of us now.

Writers are getting critiques with terms such as *post-chorus, multiple choruses*, getting asked to "lose the second verse before a chorus," "lose the bridge," and so on. Do you change the way you write to adapt? Depends.

There are a couple of schools of thought. Write what you write and write it well and its time will come around. The other is that if you want to actually make a living now from songwriting, your best chance is to follow the newest trends, but even that's not foolproof.

Here's something I've heard from many writers going to workshops and seminars or using critique services: "I'm being told to focus on what's on the radio—but at the same time told that by the time I've nailed it, radio will have changed." There's logic here. Nothing happens quickly in this process. Your song gets picked up and goes through the phases from production to release, which could be a year down the road. Not to mention the time you spent writing and pitching it. Things change. So what's your best chance of success?

Unless you're locked in with a publisher, producers, management, or the artist (your best-case scenario), you need to be writing something no one's thought of. Something so original and irresistible that all the usual suspects didn't see it first. That's going to take all the tools you have and putting whatever makes you unique in that song.

**In the end,** try not to let the other voices discourage you. If you find other people's opinions hard to deal with, just limit the listening experience to a few trusted ears. I've had songs cut that were turned down for projects, where someone loved the song but the time wasn't right. Other times, I was playing the right song for the wrong person. By all means, seek out all the wisdom you can handle, but don't lose yourself.

After that confusing trip to Nashville, Jayne not only got a couple of single song deals, but she also signed an exclusive deal with a Nashville publisher.

Sift through the advice and do what feels right.

**Seek as much wisdom as you can handle.**

**Doing it myself with a little help from my friends—in this case, old friend and super-drummer Kenny Aronoff.**

# CHAPTER 12

# DIY

There are lots of unconventional ways to get your song heard in this information age. I'm a huge fan of DIY, do it yourself.

Think of yourself as an entrepreneur. Great inventors never wait for the world to discover them; they discover things the world needs, or at least things the world's interested in.

The business model of songwriting has changed and continues to evolve. Where can you fit in? Chances are, this hasn't been part of your creative journey; maybe it hasn't had to be, but what if it were? What if you match your song with another art form? Rather than waiting on that publishing deal or for your song to be found, what if *you* get proactive?

**Before you groan** too loudly, I'm not talking about writing for the advertising world, although it's not a bad idea. What if your song is a match for a project or a product or even a campaign— but the powers that be don't know it? You can be the matchmaker.

I have a songwriter I've coached who wrote a very cool song about coffee. She didn't write it for Starbucks, but what I've suggested is that she pitch the song to a local coffee maker or coffee house. The local factor plus the relatively inexpensive cost to them to license her song can make a perfect match.

Another client in Australia sent me a song called "Stephen Hawking Wants You To." I urged her to look for any projects involving Stephen Hawking. This was before the major movie about him, *The Theory of Everything*. She reached out to a UK film company that had just done a project about him. They didn't bite, but they liked the song and opened up a dialogue about her pitching for future projects. A big open door.

She also had a very cool song called "Blue Is the Hottest Flame" but couldn't get any traction through the normal channels. I suggested she get busy Googling anything to do with the color blue near where she lives. She discovered that the local rugby team's name contained the word *blue*. She found a contact for the team's office and, very politely, emailed her idea. They were intrigued—no one had ever pitched a song to them. They set up an appointment, loved the song, and are in negotiations to use it in the team's TV advertising. This kind of a DIY idea can result in a sync usage for TV, movies, commercials, any of which can be as valuable as a traditional cut on a record.

Another writer I coach lives in Germany, has finished a jazz-influenced EP, and performs in a very popular boutique hotel in his town. I suggested he speak with the hotel owner about writing a theme for the hotel. He's done it—and the EP will be in every room of the hotel, as well as the other hotels the owner owns throughout Germany. Again, DIY pitching but money in the writer's pocket and traction.

Years before the popularity of QR Codes and Instagram, I met Ted

McConnell, who at the time was high up at Proctor and Gamble. Ted is also a songwriter. For a while, we had a very informal exchange of info. He helped me figure out how to make song coaching a reality and I helped him with his writing process. Our ideas merged one day when we had the notion of finding an unknown female country singer, writing a song that had something to do with a P&G product, and including some kind of code that would give a listener a way to download the song for free. If we could find a brand-new, signed artist, even better, but we wanted a fresh face.

We decided on Crest toothpaste, one of Proctor & Gamble's bestselling products, and I wrote two songs around the word *smile*. We got a generous budget to go for the idea and got the suits on board. Ted and I were part of a major pitch meeting with the heads of P&G in Cincinnati. The deciding vote said, "We aren't in the music business," and turned our idea down. I like to think we were ahead of our time on that one, but sooooo close.

Kye Fleming and I wrote a song in 2017 called "What Would Lennon Do." (This was around the time of the Paris nightclub shootings.) We weren't asked to write it, didn't think it had commercial hit written all over it, just wrote it to express ourselves. Rather than let it sit, we started thinking . . . big. Who might want this to be a part of their message? It's a song of peace, so we reached out to the United Nations through a client of mine who had worked at the UN. Sound far-fetched? You'd be amazed at the people who are open to a good idea. It reached all the way to the Secretary General of the UN. They loved it but only offered to put a CD of the song in their gift shop. We kept thinking.

Kye has a friend, Paula Hornick, with a connection to Amnesty International. Here's where it got really interesting.

**The song found** a home with Amnesty International, who passed it on to one of their celebrity supporters to perform on a John Lennon Tribute Concert being filmed for AMC, and then be a single the day after the show aired. My old friend Kenny Aronoff helped me get the song in front of the producers of the show. Producers agreed, contract done, one HUGE dream about to come true—except it didn't.

It's was given to Bono, Sting, Alicia Keys, John Legend, Bryan Adams, and even Yoko in the last few days. Long, long story and journey short, Amnesty was unable to get one of their artists there on the day to perform the song. Disappointed, as you can imagine, but what a ride it was!

WHAT WOULD LENNON DO
*Kye Fleming/Mark Cawley*

What if there was nothing to fight
With nothing going wrong only right
What if we imagined peace
Until it all came true

Come on WHAT WOULD LENNON DO
What if we could change how we feel
And loving everyone was for real
What if we all had a dream
A higher point of view
Come on WHAT WOULD LENNON DO

**On and on and on we go**
**Searching for a sign ... some kind of proof**
**But what if we already know and**
**What if LOVE IS ALL WE NEED ... is true**

What if words of hate disappeared . . .
Leaving us with nothing to fear
And what if we could just believe
This could all be true

Come on now what would we do
If all we need is love . . . is true

Your song might be someone's solution. Thing big, think waaaay outside the box and pitch your own song. Waiting on the world to hear you or waiting on that publisher to do the work for you is getting harder than ever. Not only that, but most of the best and most successful songwriters I know have always pitched their own ideas. They might have a great publisher, but they didn't always wait for them to come up with the best idea. They became their best promoter.

By creating a vision, you're taking control of your songs, you're taking control of your career, and the buzz you get from connecting your vision to someone else's can be bigger than you ever imagined. Control equals freedom, and freedom is one of the reasons you're on this journey.

**Your song might be
someone's solution.**

**Brenda Russell, on my left, is one of my favorite people on the planet and one of my three dream co-writers. Connecting here with Chaka Khan in London.**

# CHAPTER 13

# ORGANIC NETWORKING

Many of us songwriters are introverts. Let's face it. If you're working in solitude, collecting your thoughts, and trying to channel that perfect melody, you're not doing it in an office surrounded by people. (Unless you're working on Nashville's Music Row, and even there, it's the same but different.) I don't think of writing as a group effort, but I do think of the music business like a team sport.

This is where the attributes of being an introvert, the stuff that allows you to dig deep, goes from being an asset to a detriment. We write in a vacuum, but your aim is to show your baby to the whole wide world. We need someone to sing our praises and, most of all, we need someone to sing our songs! How are they going to hear them?

It's getting harder and harder to be an introvert in the music business. There was a time when a songwriter worked his or her magic, passed the song over to a publisher, the publisher played it for a label, producer, or artist, and they recorded it. The songwriter only had to get dressed to go to the mailbox to pick up the ASCAP check or go to an award ceremony to get whatever you call the shiny thing you take home.

Perfect job for the Howard Hughes in all of us. I just don't believe that model exists anymore.

**"**

**I don't think of writing as a group effort, but I do think of the music business like a team sport.**

**"**

**We introverts tend** to close our eyes and click our heels three times when we hear the term *network*. Take me anywhere but there! *My stuff is personal, they won't get it . . . don't want to hear a critique, don't want to hear words like* nice *. . . I just want a YES. Preferably via text.*

But it takes a village to raise a hit single. While a good publisher might give you the space you need to do what you do, and not have to do the things you don't, these publishers are few and far between. Really far between. These days, they want to see a writer who can bring more. Can they play live? Can they self-promote? Can they make contacts on their own? Can they work social media? Can they discover other writers to write with? Can they forge a friendship with a producer/artist/manager? Can they bring their own funding?

The good news? You can still be introverted and succeed. The internet is the first tool for that. You can create a platform, website, fan page, and fan base all while wearing the same old shorts and ball cap you wore when you wrote the song. You can reach out and not leave home. You can network that way. But . . .

From personal experience, I know there's just no substitute for "old school" networking. Going out to hear live music, connecting with other songwriters and artists. Touching base with everyone you know in the business, keeping your name in front of someone, even when doing that seems sort of creepy by an introvert's standards. Self-promotion is hard for most. In my career, I've always had sort of a grudging respect for the networking writers. Some were more networker than songwriter, some a hybrid; *those* are the ones who seemed to be incredibly successful in the music business.

I will share with you that I fell somewhere in between over a long career. I networked as much as I was comfortable with but probably not enough. Didn't like to attend dinners, parties, or events . . . unless I was getting one of those shiny things I mentioned earlier. I missed out on some great opportunities by not "putting myself out there," but I felt I could only do what I do well on my own terms. I was lucky to find a good team before the era of free agency.

**“**

**It takes a village to
raise a hit single.**

**”**

If you're writing great songs and you're a people person, go for it, because no one will ever care quite as much about your career as you. Self-promotion is not just for recording artists; it's for songwriters, too.

Creating contacts and being able to use them is usually a result of good networking. It might be unconscious networking, but it's networking just the same. The co-writer you had, the songwriter you met in an online songwriting group, the guitar player you know, your best friends' friend who works in an entertainment law firm in New York—these all become part of your songwriting path. Think of them as an organic network.

So many of the contacts in my songwriting life started with the smallest of connections. These have proven to be the gift that keeps on giving. Quite a few friends I made in the beginning of my career are friends to this day. I didn't give much thought at the time to growing old with these folks. That's not on your radar when you're out to conquer the world. But looking through my contact list, I see I'm still in touch with many of them today.

Here's how this all can work: One of my first managers, Joe Halderman, introduced me to Peter Frampton, for whom Faith Band opened. Terry Barnes, who worked with Joe, is the brother of Faith Band drummer Dave Barnes, with whom I played. Terry ended up President and CEO of Ticketmaster and introduced me to one of my songwriting heroes, Lowell George of Little Feat.

There are the guys in Faith Band with whom I shared a lot of stages as I accumulated my 10,000 hours of expertise in this game.

John Cooper was the sound man for Faith Band. He now mixes Bruce Springsteen all around the world. John introduced me to Wynonna Judd. One of my good buddies, Bob Britt, played on my home demos years ago. Bob and John Cooper eventually worked together with Wynonna. I send many of my coaching clients to Bob for his demo production.

Then there's Torquil Creevy, whom I first met in England when I was an artist signed to Riva Records. Torquil moved on to Miles Copeland's publishing company and offered me a deal when he got there. This led to attending Miles's writer retreats in the South of France, and those contacts led to meeting some wonderful writers who are in my contacts still. He introduced me to songwriter Billy Lawrie, who introduced me to his sister Lulu. The "To Sir with Love" Lulu. Billy, Lulu, and I wrote "My Angel Is Here" on Wynonna's awesome album *Revelations*. Torquil also introduced me to Nick Battle at Windswept Pacific Music, who signed me and got some of my best cuts including "Wayward Soul" recorded by Joe Cocker on his platinum album *Across from Midnight*.

Some of my favorite co-writers and friends were introduced to me by another connection. Most writers I know are good like that. Kye Fleming introduced me to all things Nashville. I connected

Kye with Brenda Russell—we wrote "Dancing in My Dreams" for
Tina Turner. Brenda introduced me to Diane Warren and Baby-
face. She also introduced me to Chaka Khan, who recorded our
song "Dare You to Love Me." Countless connections that have
lasted through the years. Brenda even introduced me to Lisa
Fischer—who introduced me to . . . the Stones. I have to tell you, I
grew up a huge Stones fan, even joined their fan club—the sticker
is still on the back of their first album. Lisa had been singing background with the Stones for years and not only invited my wife
and me backstage but also took us "backstage backstage" to the
Stones' inner sanctum to meet the boys. I was a fourteen-year-old
kid again when Lisa introduced me to Keith and Ronnie by saying,
"Guys, you must know Mark. He's a great songwriter." I got the
introduction from heaven but, to this day, I don't recall what I
said in return. I do remember looking over at Mick while we were
having wine and getting a nod hello. Lisa, I will love you forever.

It's just as important to *continue* to stay in touch with your connections as it is to *make* them in the first place. Cultivate the
friendships; touch base from time to time. Keep your info up-
dated. You never know where one of your old friends will land in
this business, and someone you shared a moment with years ago
can easily reenter your universe.

I'm not suggesting you "work" your contacts as much as work at
keeping up with them. Along with your family and your talent,
they're the most valuable asset you have.

**Leaving the nest** is the "tipping point" for most writers, myself included. As a young writer, I headed to New York, Boston,
Indianapolis, Los Angeles, London, and finally Nashville. It was
hard, but I dug in. Learned from everyone I could, read every

book, played every bar, wrote with anyone who asked. Anything to just be able to call myself a songwriter and believe it. Every name went into my book.

One of the first co-writes I had after coming to Nashville was with a terrific country writer named Kerry Kurt Phillips. Kerry wrote some classic country songs including "I Don't Need Your Rockin' Chair" for George Jones. I don't even remember what we wrote that day, but we had a fun time realizing how many friends we had in common. As I was leaving, I said, "Man, it's a small world," to which he added, "but I wouldn't want to paint it."

**❝**

**No one will ever care quite as much about your career as you.**

**❞**

**Young McCartney searching for his Lennon, 1967, Endwell, New York.**

# CHAPTER 14

# CO-WRITING

**Until now,** we've been talking about writing *your* song. I've talked about the tools you need to flesh out *your* lyric, find *your* melody, make *your* demo, promote *your* songs, and take *your* meeting. Up until now, it's been *your* solitary journey. What if you had help? What if instead of looking for that muse, you had one in the room with you? Flesh and blood, living, breathing—a like-minded fellow traveler? In other words, a co-writer. Co-writing is such a part of the new normal for songwriters that we'll spend the next two chapters on it.

Like most songwriters starting out, I thought writing was a thing you did with a guitar and a pen, in your room, alone with your thoughts. That was a big part of the draw in those formative years—it was a way to express myself. Writing always seemed like the natural next step after learning to play an instrument; learning those Beatles songs and then making up my own. And for an introverted fifteen-year-old, a great way to meet girls. Carrying around a guitar was one thing, but making up words . . . well, that was deep. At least that's what I was going for. I read the back of every record. I knew John had Paul, Mick had Keith, Carol had Gerry, Elton had Bernie, Burt had Hal, Holland had Dozier and one more Holland, Smokey had . . . I don't know if Smokey had a co-writer, but he was awesome. I knew there was more than one name on those songwriting credits, but the idea of finding someone to write my songs with was a long way off.

I had grown up in the garage band era. Not the Apple DAW (Digital Audio Workstation) Garageband, I mean four guys making noise in my parents' garage. That kind of garage band. We'd learn the songs by most of the bands we'd seen on Ed Sullivan the Sunday before and do our best to look all British. But none of us was really writing songs, and we definitely were not writing songs that could stand next to those classics.

I started making up my own because most of those songs on the radio were too hard for a self-taught, pimply-faced, fifteen-year-old, fake British rock star to play. I became the guy in the band who would bring in ideas we could make our own. Since I was that smart guy, I also got the other jobs the band guys didn't want to mess with, such as making out set lists and writing our band propaganda.

I grew up alongside some good players, but I never found the Lennon to my McCartney. I learned by writing an endless stream of derivative pop songs, by myself for the most part, and I'm thankful for that. I had to learn how to put a complete song together all by myself.

Slowly, the songs I was writing were getting better, and so were the bands. From my first one, no lie . . . put your hands together for the Patagonianists. Yep. That band lasted one night—one gig at my high school dance in Endwell, New York. That begot the Basket of Flowers, who begot Standing Room Only, who begot Beggar's Opera (a really good band with multiple songwriters but still, no co-writing), and finally Indiana-based Faith Band and actually making records with my songs on them.

John Cascella was the other main songwriter in that group, and he was a huge talent and a beautiful guy. John went on to play in John Mellencamp's band and single-handedly made the accordion cool again. Carl Storie was the singer and occasional songwriter for Faith, having written the band's only hit, "Dancing Shoes." Having a great voice like Carl's was a bonus for any songwriter. We also had a terrific blues-based guitarist, Dave Bennett, and a rock-solid drummer, Dave Barnes.

I will always be grateful to all the guys in all the bands that not only encouraged me to write songs but were also willing to play and record some of them.

Carl and I recorded an album under the name "Blinding Tears" with a bunch of my songs, but that was my swan song as an artist. It was full-on songwriting for other artists after that one. By the early '90s, I was having some success with songs I'd written with others, such as "Heaven Come Down," co-written with Bill Baker. It went to number one in Sweden with Jennifer Brown. I also had one I wrote on my own, one of my favorite songs, "Dance with a Stranger," recorded by Taylor Dayne on her *Soul Dancing* album. *Soul Dancing* earned my first gold record award.

My publisher began suggesting co-writers for me to meet with. I was wide open to the idea and jumped in. Some of these were blind dates with all that conjures up: apprehension, fear, and once in a while, a dream date. The first one that I really clicked with was Shelly Peiken, an LA transplant from New York who came to my house in Indiana to write for a few days. We wrote three songs, and I have to say, she was more accomplished at this co-writing thing than I was, but she was gracious and made the idea of writing with someone else in the room not only doable, but also a fun experience. She remains a friend to this day as well as a hugely successful songwriter and, now, author of the Grammy-nominated (spoken word) "Confessions of a Serial Songwriter." But the real eye-opening co-writing epiphany was still around the corner.

Torquil Creevy was running Miles Copeland's publishing company, Bugle Songs, and responsible for signing me as the first nonartist at Bugle. Up until then, Miles's company was responsible for Sting's catalog as well as the songs of Squeeze, REM, the Bangles, and many of his IRS label artists. The idea of a stand-alone songwriter, someone not making records and not in a band, was new to Miles, but Torquil was a real champion in getting me signed and promoted. Part of that mission was to get me co-writing with successful writers. I had recently decided to move with my wife and two young daughters back to Indiana to take a breather from the music business in LA and was now just a five-hour car trip from Nashville. We agreed it was the perfect place to expand my network of songwriters.

**Torquil set me up** in a house on Lombardy Street in the Green Hills area of Nashville for a few days. The first day of co-writing was with Mary Ann Kennedy, part of the duo Kennedy Rose signed to Sting's label, Pangæa. Mary Ann is a force of nature: voice of an angel and can play anything with strings. She had had some major country hits but also had a very cool pop edge to her writing. I had brought down my usual tools: computer, electric guitar, and amp along with a keyboard with some drum loops. She brought a beautiful Everly Brothers black Gibson acoustic and . . . Kye Fleming.

There are days we can all look back at and know they were seismic events: meeting my wife, Kathy, for example, and seeing my daughters Taylor and Morgan for the first time. On my songwriting journey, the earth shook when I first met Kye. Kye had been a three-time BMI Writer of the Year. "I Was Country When Country Wasn't Cool" is just one of her iconic hits. Turns out I was renting Kye's house. She and Mary Ann were tight and wrote together a bunch. On this day, she had just come along to see if everything was OK with the house and intended to leave Mary Ann and me to it.

All I remember of that moment is I started playing something on guitar, very Roy Orbison-influenced, Mary Ann jumped in, and Kye sat down and watched in a chair in the corner, wearing a great smile. Kye stayed and then eased into the song. The three of us wrote a song called "For Love Alone" that day and became instant best friends. All of us brought something different to the table, including matching wicked senses of humor.

That co-write led to dinner and the next day a frantic search for a place to record this song we all loved. Kye and Mary Ann opened up their world, shared their connections, and in a few days, we wrote a couple of songs that are among my favorites to this day. Without them, I don't know if I could have envisioned myself and my family moving to Nashville. Because of them, we did.

That experience began a season of writing for the three of us that produced some distinctive songs. It was what great co-writing should be: unselfish, open, fun, and uninhibited. We felt we had invented something that was bigger than us and the perfect sum of our parts—what I later learned was perfect co-writing. We had a few successes, including "You Are to Me" on Rick Trevino's gold album *Looking for the Light.*, "The End of the Line" for Kathy Mattea featuring Michael McDonald, and a song that really was the end of the line for Russ Taff called "Love Is Not a Thing." (He's a huge star in Christian music, but our song was the first single from his foray into country. After it stalled, he went back to Christian music.)

Kye and I went on to write a bunch more, including "Dancing in My Dreams" for Tina Turner. We still write together when the spirit moves us. She made the Nashville Songwriters Hall of Fame recently. She is truly awesome and one of my dream co-writers.

**Great co-writing should be:
unselfish, open, fun, and uninhibited.**

# CHAPTER 15

# MEET YOUR CO-WRITER

**Co-writer Kye Fleming opened up Nashville for me.**

**(L to R) Mary Ann Kennedy, Jess Leary, Marc Beeson, Emmylou Harris, Renee Armond, unknown session engineer, Ashley Cleveland, Pam Rose, Kye Fleming, and me. Nashville, Tennessee.**

Before you start to work, meet your potential co-writer. Have a cup of coffee or a drink. It's a lot like dating—see if you have anything in common before you spend a long day in a room together. It's not foolproof. I've made some great friends this way who didn't turn out to be great co-writers, and I've also written some of my favorite songs with writers who, on paper, didn't seem like a match.

If you're booking these writing sessions yourself or you're having a publisher set you up, you're looking for magic. You want to be compatible, but you don't want someone who only does what you do. You're each hoping the other brings something to the table. Again, kind of like dating and marriage—looking to complement each other, sum is better than the parts, all that stuff.

Co-writing is continuing to evolve with some current pop and country hits sporting anywhere from four to seven credited writers. How does that happen? The artist is involved, a track guy might be providing the needed vibe, maybe a few top liners (more on these writers later), possibly another song being sampled where all those writers are credited. It can get crazy. It can also be a case of writers looking for pure volume. You can find writers booking three sessions a day in Nashville, and the more people in the room, the quicker it might get written.

This is important: know going in that the credit will be split evenly between the people in the room, no matter who does what in the end. That's a hard one for new writers to swallow, but hey, do it long enough and it evens out, I promise. Some days, you feel like you wrote a song on your own and the other writers watched. Other days, you're buying lunch and encouraging them to "keep at it; you're on fire!"

**Nashville is known** for its fair splits; other markets can get trickier. I've written in the UK and other countries and had someone call later to clarify and approve the split, $21\frac{1}{3}$ percent for me, $23\frac{2}{3}$ percent for the other guy, and the rest for the artist who was on the phone for most of the good stuff. A lesson for me early on was to talk about the expectation of the split prior to the co-writing session. I had a friend who had their co-writer's assistant call them after reviewing an audiotape of the day and breaking it down to whose ideas ended up where. It can get ugly unless you decide up front. If there are no publishers involved, it's best to just work it out in that coffee conversation before you actually write. The alternative is to use a simple split agreement the day of your writing session. This is a common form you can download. God forbid the song gets some action before everybody is on the same page.

On the day of the co-write, it never hurts to come prepared with a couple of titles, concepts, or a bit of a melody, but it's really about listening to each other and creating something new and exciting together. A big no-no for me would be the co-writer who comes in intent on working on their idea right from the start or, even worse, wants me to help them finish something they already had started.

What happens if you throw out that million-dollar title or melody you've been saving, and your co-writer turns it into small change? Can you go rewrite it with someone else? No. I know it's hurts but . . . NO. You could call them and ask, but the reality is, your reputation is built around your integrity and creativity. If your co-writer thinks you're going to write the same idea with three other writers, it won't be long before you're one lonely writer. This is why you have a coffee meeting; you try your best to put your ideas in the right hands. Pretend you're picking a babysitter for little Dylan. Would you leave him with just anybody?

I know writers like to say their songs are their children. I have children; they're not songs.

Do your homework on co-writers, don't be too precious, trust your gut, and hope for a little magic. Learn how your co-writer tends to process information. Just ask them. Do they need quiet periods to gather their thoughts, or are they the kind of writer who needs constant stimulus? You can set yourself up for an awkward co-writing experience by not being in tune with your new friend. Make sure you can laugh with them. Pick up the tab once in a while and show up on time. Writers like that.

I've written about some of my great co-writing sessions. Now let me take you to a bad co-writing session and how to handle it.

**Make sure you can laugh with them. Pick up the tab once in a while and show up on time. Writers like that.**

## THE DAY

If you write long enough, it's going to happen. It happened to me more times than I can remember. It happens to every writer I know. It happens to writers I'm coaching. It's happening right now on Music Row, in New York, in LA, and in London.

Your publisher or a friend sets you up on a "blind date" to co-write. Everybody has high hopes. You're prepared, maybe you've even been able to hear some of the songs this new friend has written, and you're excited, nervous even, but this is what you do.

9:00 A.M.
You get your stories out of the way, what one of my buddies always called having your "pissing contest," where you let each other know what you've written in the past.

10:00 A.M.
Down to it. One of you throws out an idea and . . . nothing. The other tries a riff/groove/potential title and . . . still nothing. Lunch is already starting to look like a good idea. This is when you hope your partner has a great sense of humor and that you haven't lost yours. After all, in the words of John Hiatt, "What's the worst that can happen—they put me in songwriter jail?"

11:30 A.M.
Hopefully, your new co-writer is a good hang because you still got nothing.

12:00 P.M.
Lunch!

1:00 P.M.
You're more comfortable with each other. Back to work and . . . nothing. It dawns on both of you that this isn't going anywhere.

4:00 P.M.
You give it your best, wrap it up, maybe blame it on an off day, and agree to try again. But chances are, you won't because you'd rather set yourself on fire than go through that again.

2:00 A.M. LYING AWAKE QUESTIONS

How can you avoid this next time? Once again, it helps to spend time with your co-writer before your session, if possible. Coffee, drinks, a meal—anything to get a sense of chemistry. It helps to work with someone who doesn't do what you do. I've had a few sessions where a publisher thought I'd love working with a particular writer, only to find out we basically do the same thing. The co-writes that have been magic for me have always been with someone with a different approach, and we end up complementing each other. We come up with some magic that neither of us could have done on our own. It will happen. You may just have to suffer through speed date hell to find the love of your life.

In the end, you need the mentality that the great New York Yankee closer Mariano Rivera had. You're going to lose one once in a while, but you have to put it out of your mind and pitch tomorrow. Don't let it shake your confidence.

Chalk it up to experience, find more great ideas, book more co-writes, and one of these sessions will be pure magic.

## THE FIVE CO-WRITING FEARS

When I coach songwriters who are new to the idea of co-writing, I hear these fears all the time:

- My idea is crap!
- They'll take my idea and turn it into something I'll hate.
- They'll laugh at me.
- No one else could possibly understand me.
- No one will ever want to co-write with me again!

Maybe the biggest motivator for me was when I started writing with writers I admired. Sure, you learn, but you also find they're just as scared of the Five Co-writing Fears as you are from time to time, and that helps. As you begin to come up with ideas that aren't crap, your co-writer takes your idea and makes it better. You share a few laughs, they "get" you, and . . . you get to write with more good songwriters.

How do you up the odds of a great song coming out of your co-write? First and foremost, seek out good people to work with. To quote my friend Ed Hill's country hit, "Most People Are Good," and so are most songwriters. Find ones who are on your same level, same path. Joining songwriting groups can be a great way of losing your fear of sharing. Just by hearing other writers talk about their process, you gain insight into yourself. You're not alone, not by a long shot.

Sharing your song ideas might still be a leap of faith, but try it. If you stay open and give your best every time, you'll have more great days co-writing than bad ones. Promise.

The kind of co-writer I wish for you is number two on my holy trinity of co-writers: Brenda Russell. Brenda is one of those touched-by-the-hand-of-God songwriters, and I thank Him for putting us together. She's a co-writer of the music for *The Color Purple* on Broadway, a Tony and Grammy winner, and a lifelong inspiration.

I was on Miles Copeland's songwriting retreat in the Dordogne Valley region of France. This was the third writer's retreat I had attended, each one awe-inspiring. I wrote with a different group each day for two weeks, a Cordon Bleu-trained chef prepared our meals, there was all that wonderful French wine, and . . . I slept in a castle. At this very retreat, Kevin Savigar, Patty Smyth, Brenda

Russell, Bruce Roberts, and I wrote a song that turned out to be a hit single for soft jazz superstar Tom Scott called "Don't Get Any Better than This." You can imagine where that muse came from.

**As good as it was,** one day prior to writing that song, I found myself a little stir crazy and wanting to get "off the ranch" for a bit when Torquil (there he is again) mentioned that he was headed to the Bordeaux airport to pick up Brenda Russell and bring her into the camp. Did I fancy riding along? He had me at Bordeaux, because I knew there'd be a fine dinner thrown in. We were off.

Now, I had heard some of Brenda's music, loved "Piano in the Dark" and "Get Here," but we'd never met. When we picked her up, it was as if we all had been friends for years.

After dinner the next day, I went into the writing room I had used earlier and just started playing. I had brought along a state-of-the-art Kurzweil keyboard loaded with loops. As was pretty much my go-to method back then, I just let the loop play and created an atmospheric vibe using some pads from the Kurzweil library.

I thought I was all alone until I felt somebody standing in the doorway. There was Brenda, who smiled and said, "That, my friend, is some funky shit!" The next day, we wrote a song with a writer/artist named Vinx who had been in Sting's band. The three of us came up with a song called "Don't You Talk to Me like That." It would not only go on a Vinx album but also appeared as a single on Will Downing's top three jazz album *Sensual Journey*. It was the start of a beautiful, creative relationship between Brenda and me that included cuts by Joe Cocker, Tina Turner, Chaka Khan, and a few on Brenda's solo albums.

# CHAPTER 16

# LEARNING A FOREIGN LANGUAGE

**Del Newman conducting my song "PCH 101"
with the London Symphony Orchestra in 1985.**

How important is it for you as a songwriter to be able to speak different languages? I'm not talking about fluent French, although it would have come in handy when I was trying to ask directions in the Paris Metro.

It's easy to Google anything we're interested in to get a few of the basics. It helps to know a few terms before taking your car in for repair, a little about the stock market if you hope to hang on to those future royalties, or even insight into what your colon does before you go in for that . . . -oscopy thing. Knowledge is power; even a little can help you be heard and be in the conversation.

**If you're a songwriter** and you're headed into the studio to work with a producer or engineer, you stand a better chance of being happy with the outcome if you can talk some tech talk. If you're strictly a lyricist and you're writing with a melody person, it's great if you can talk in their terms about what you like or don't like. Maybe as simple as seventh chords, major versus minor changes, inversions, lifts. It may not be your thing, but it's theirs, and helping them help you helps the song in the end.

If you write on guitar and don't have a talent for writing lyrics, you can still help steer the direction by being able to use terminology familiar to the lyricist in the room. Sometimes just being able to point out what's *not* working for you is key: rhyme scheme, not enough detail, anything is better than saying, "I don't like it, but I can't begin to tell you why."

I've directed some of my songwriting clients to classes such as "Piano for Songwriters" or "Guitar for Songwriters," even vocal lessons for a lyric writer. The point is, the more song elements you're familiar with, the better you can articulate your thoughts toward the song's creation and production.

I've written songs with quite a few artists, and many times they would start by telling me they weren't really songwriters, but they could tell you about the songs that moved them and why—maybe not in the most technical terms, but by talking about another artist's song and why the chorus was so great, or why the groove worked for them. The more they could explain, the bigger their role would be in creating the song.

I started in bands and early on did a recording session in New York City with the legendary Eddie Kramer, who had engineered Jimi Hendrix. I don't remember much of the session or how my little band got in front of him, but I do remember feeling like I had no business saying anything. Looking back, it *was* my business to speak up, no matter my level of studio expertise. It was at least partly my music and my (albeit limited) vision. Eddie knew Eddie but didn't know Mark. He did an amazing job of making my band sound good. But how much better might the session have been if I could have confidently shown him my inspirations? Maybe played a record or two that I loved? Showed him what I was shooting for?

**Overcoming fear** is a biggie for artists and songwriters; knowledge goes a long way to helping you become fearless. The musicians, songwriters, and music business people I've run into not only are great about sharing their knowledge but also willing to learn something from a novice. I'm talking the been-there-done-that kind of pros. They tend to be secure enough that they don't make you feel foolish for not knowing the exact right word to describe that vibe you're going for. If you have made an effort to be able to communicate and speak their language, it's a beautiful thing. It's a respect thing.

Carl Storie and I were in London recording our album *Blinding Tears* in 1985. Our producer was an Englishman named John Eden.

I had written a song called "PCH 101" and desperately wanted a string section on it. John asked whom I'd like to have do the arrangement. It wasn't going to be me. I threw out the names of the two arrangers I knew had written and conducted the string arrangements for some of my favorite Elton John songs—Paul Buckmaster and Del Newman. A few weeks later, John informed me Del took the job and was working on "PCH 101."

Fast forward to the later days of the project. My wife, Kathy, and I were standing in a studio in London while Del Newman was on the podium conducting the arrangement of my song with a large string section from the London Symphony Orchestra. Absolutely one of my favorite moments in life. After a couple of run-throughs, he stopped and asked me what I thought and did I have any suggestions? This time, I did have a few thoughts. I had listened to "Madman across the Water" and "Tiny Dancer" and was able to share some thoughts on moments that moved me in those arrangements. He conveyed my ideas to the players, and I loved the result. Del could have been resentful and aloof with this pop songwriter who couldn't read music. Instead, he made me feel like a collaborator, like we were speaking the same language.

**The more song elements you're familiar with, the better you can articulate your thoughts.**

# CHAPTER 17

# THE ARTIST/ SONGWRITER

**With one of my all-time favorite artists and songwriters, Glenn Tilbrook from Squeeze.**

This topic might seem like a nonstarter in a book on songwriting. After all, wouldn't all the same tools apply? Yes and no.

The tools I've been sharing on how to write the best songs you possibly can will work for songwriters, singer-songwriters, and artists—with one possible exception. If you're an aspiring artist, your goal is a record deal in whatever form—major label, indy, or self-release—and you might not be as concerned with writing a song that another artist could record. You might be thinking, "I'm writing this for myself, not thinking hit singles, making a statement for who I am as an artist." If this is the case, you might be writing more introspective, highly personal songs or even songs that are more "your heart than their charts." This is great. If anything, you have more freedom because you know who's going to record your songs—you.

**But consider this.** Lots of artists started as songwriters. They were always on the artist path but got their career jump-started by other artists recording their songs: Lady Gaga, Julia Michaels, Brandy Clark, Bruno Mars, Chris Stapleton, Natalie Hemby, Lori McKenna, even as far back as Neil Diamond and Barry Manilow. It's a win-win for a songwriter pursuing an artist career if another artist takes your song places you haven't been yet. This can get you noticed in a hurry in LA, New York, London, and Nashville, and not just by the powers that be but also by fans. A tribe takes pride knowing an artist they follow had their songs cut first by another artist.

I started as an artist, but once a few major artists gave me the chance to write for them, my whole career changed. I left the artist world to write full time for others. Doesn't mean that should be your path. Even though writing for artists who didn't normally write their own songs was the way forward for me, I still tend to lean toward artists who do write their own songs. It feels more personal. Sounds like I'm kicking the very people who had given me a living, but there's a distinction. Tina Turner, Joe Cocker, Diana Ross, and Chaka Khan are artists, but the driving factor for them is they're *performers* first and foremost. The other big deciding factor to me was the complete freedom. I don't have an identity or image as a songwriter. I can be a chameleon. I've had songs recorded in pop, rock, contemporary jazz, country, and Christian genres, and that has been a source of personal pride for me.

The Peter Frampton "nobody" story in the introduction was an early glimpse into my dilemma of whether to be a songwriter or an artist. On May 25, 1975, my band Faith opened up for Fleetwood Mac in South Bend, Indiana, at the C. Morris Civic Center. It wasn't sold out, but that night the Mac was everything you know them as today. Tremendous players and charisma to burn. Lindsey Buckingham and Stevie Nicks were new to the band, but it was all in place. They were touring behind the *Fleetwood Mac* album with Mick and John on the cover. They played what became classics: "Rhiannon," "Over My Head," and "Say You Love Me."

I watched them from backstage and thought, "There it is." Up close: star power, great songs, the whole package. I lay awake that night thinking, "Am I as good as that?" "Is our band as good as that one?" "Do I want it the way they obviously do? Because if I don't, I'm not going to get it. I might get a taste of it, but I'm not going to keep it."

It was a real gut-check moment. Even though I've been around and written with some of the best songwriters on the planet, the artist path is a different deal. I could hone the craft. I can't manufacture the charisma. Being a songwriter—a "nobody"—was looking better. I had the same feeling opening up for Journey, Rush, the Doobie Brothers, and even lesser-known artists such as Rory Gallager and Thin Lizzy. They wanted all of it. I wasn't sure I did. And that meant I wouldn't get it.

In a town like Nashville, you'll also find some amazing writers who came to be that way by a failing artist career. Artistry is what brought them here, but their album went nowhere. That can be hard to imagine when you hear songwriters do their songs better than the record you know, but it just might not have been their time.

Brett James is a hugely successful Nashville writer who had a couple of record deals. Seems like a can't-miss, but so many factors go into an artist's success. One star doesn't want to align with the rest, and it just doesn't happen.

I've written with Sarah Buxton and, more than anyone else in Nashville, felt she was a star in waiting: great singer, beautiful, and a great songwriter. Everybody could see it. She recorded two projects, but the timing just wasn't right. She's had a solid career as a writer including a song I love, "Stupid Boy," a hit for Keith Urban. She is doing a record as I write this, and I wouldn't be surprised to see her fly as an artist this time.

**Once in a while**, you read an interview with a successful songwriter where they admit they're much happier writing songs than they would have been as an artist. There are also a few—and I might fall into this category—who feel they might not have survived the star trip. So many of the ones I know personally have sacrificed families and loved ones in search of stardom. I'm glad I didn't have to, but I love the gifts true artists give us and appreciate the sacrifice involved.

If you're an artist and a songwriter and you live and breathe it, by all means go for it. Write great songs, and if along the way other people want to record them, let them. If your artist path takes off to the point where you should keep your best songs for yourself, fantastic. Until then, let somebody love them, record them, and shine a light back to you.

**"**

**I love the gifts true artists give us and appreciate the sacrifice involved.**

**"**

| Rank | | Title / Artist |
|---|---|---|
| 1 | NEW | DAY & NIGHT |
| 2 | | DON'T CALL ME BABY |
| 3 | | OOPS!...I DID IT AGAIN |
| 4 | | SEX BOMB |
| 5 | NEW | MASTERBLASTER 2000 |
| 6 | | THE BAD TOUCH |
| 7 | | HEART OF ASIA |
| 8 | | BOUND 4 DA RELOAD (CASUALTY) |
| 9 | NEW | LUVSTRUCK |
| 10 | | KOOCHY |
| 11 | | TOCA'S MIRACLE |
| 12 | | THONG SONG |
| 13 | | TELL ME WHY (THE RIDDLE) |
| 14 | NEW | WALKING ON WATER |
| 15 | NEW | IMPOSSIBLE |
| 16 | | FILL ME IN |
| 17 | | THE WICKER MAN |
| 18 | | HE WASN'T MAN ENOUGH |
| 19 | | ACHILLES HEEL |
| 20 | | MAMBO ITALIANO |
| 21 | | FLOWERS |
| 22 | NEW | BLUE TOMORROW |
| 23 | | PROUD |
| 24 | | PRIVATE EMOTION |
| 25 | | CRAZY LOVE |
| 26 | | BLOW YA MIND |
| 27 | | BUGGIN |
| 28 | | AMAZED |
| 29 | NEW | THEME FROM GUTBUSTER |
| 30 | | SHORTY (GOT HER EYES ON ME) |
| 31 | | NEVER BE THE SAME AGAIN |
| 32 | | CANDY |
| 33 | NEW | IS THAT YOUR FINAL ANSWER? |
| 34 | NEW | DON'T PLAY THAT SONG AGAIN |
| 35 | | DIRTY WATER |
| 36 | | SAY MY NAME |
| 37 | NEW | (FRIDAY NIGHT) |
| 38 | | DEEPER SHADE OF BLUE |
| 39 | | JUST AROUND THE HILL |
| 40 | | AUTOPHILIA |
| 41 | NEW | THE GAMES WE PLAY |
| 42 | NEW | ANGRY SKIES |
| 43 | | SMOOTH |
| 44 | | I WANNA LOVE YOU FOREVER |
| 45 | NEW | ACCESS |
| 46 | | PER SEMPRE AMORE (FOREVER IN LOVE) |
| 47 | | A SONG FOR THE LOVERS |
| 48 | | BIG GIRL |
| 49 | NEW | SLEEPING WITH VICTOR |
| 50 | | FUNKY MUSIC |
| 51 | | BREATHE |
| 52 | NEW | FOOL FOR LOVE |
| 53 | | FOOL AGAIN |
| 54 | | CRY |
| 55 | | DON'T WANNA LET YOU GO |
| 56 | | DON'T GIVE UP |
| 57 | | AFTER LOVE |
| 58 | | THE TIME IS NOW |
| 59 | NEW | FREAKIN' IT |
| 60 | | YOU SEE THE TROUBLE WITH ME |
| 61 | | ALL THE SMALL THINGS |
| 62 | NEW | RUNNIN |
| 63 | | WHO FEELS LOVE? |
| 64 | | CAUGHT OUT THERE |
| 65 | | STILL |
| 66 | | PURE SHORES |
| 67 | | STILL D.R.E. |
| 68 | | BAG IT UP |
| 69 | | FEELING THIS WAY |
| 70 | | AMERICAN PIE |
| 71 | | DAILY |
| 72 | | FREAKYTIME |
| 73 | | RAP SUPERSTAR/ROCK SUPERSTAR |
| 74 | RE | JUMP DOWN |
| 75 | | THE BEST IS YET TO COME |

**This one debuted at number ONE!**

# CHAPTER 18

# HOW TO WRITE A HIT

I can almost hear the groans: "Who is this guy? How can he claim to know how to write a hit? And if he knows, how come he hasn't written hundreds of them?"

**No one can guarantee** a hit. No label, no producer, no artist, and no songwriter. Max Martin misses, Diane Warren misses, Ryan Tedder misses. They all miss more often than they hit. There is no formula. But there are things you can do to up the odds of your song getting heard, cut, and if all the stars align, becoming a hit.

Start by doing your homework. Listen to the hits and look for patterns. Are you hearing more and more songs about affirmation? I want to see you be brave, strong, beautiful, happy? Since the beginning, songwriters have known one of the quickest ways to a listener's heart is to lift them up with your song. There's a fancy term called second-person positive, basically a lyric that makes someone else feel great about themselves. If there's a tried-and-true version of this, it's the old Joe Cocker standard, written by Billy Preston and Bruce Fisher, "You Are So Beautiful."

Every publisher, producer, and artist in Nashville is always asking for "up-tempo positive." The reason for this is the sheer volume of ballads and mid-tempos they get. When a couple of writers get in the room with an acoustic guitar or a piano, they seem to turn into Joni Mitchell or James Taylor. Hard to create the energy needed unless you plan for it. But again, your chances of getting that hit improve by giving the powers that be what they're asking for.

One of the very best ways I know is to get in the habit of deconstructing current hits. Go beyond just learning to play them; do things like write down the structure, print out the lyric, and make notes about the production. I'm always amazed at the songwriting clients I get who will say they want to write a huge song but pay absolutely no attention to current hits. If you're writing pop or even new country and are still creating long intros, lots of verses, using only one hook, and aren't familiar with terms such as *post-chorus*, you might have a harder road.

Try going one step beyond deconstructing and create a playlist with a couple of hits along with a song of your own. Try to pick songs that might have something in common with yours, but the idea is to be objective. Does your song hold up to the others? If not, why? Go back to your notes. What's different? The point is not to clone but to get this info into your subconscious so the next song you write is at least informed by structural ideas that are more current.

Even though you're listening to the radio and learning the structural and lyrical as well as musical content, remember the songs you're hearing were probably written and recorded as much as a year ago or more. If you set out to write something exactly like what you're hearing, you're likely too late. So what can you do now?

Try to take it all in and then add yourself to the mix. What makes you different as a songwriter? Can you bring something fresh to your songwriting? You could argue there's nothing new under the sun, but I disagree. Music goes in cycles, styles change, and old becomes new every once in a while. Our job is to tap into a listener's head and create something a whole lot of people love at the same time. It's not easy, but the chances get better not only by honing your craft, but also by learning what came before (even if that's only a month back). It all goes into your toolbox as a songwriter and gives you the best chance of writing a hit.

I want to talk about the biggest obstacle for solo songwriters. This comes up in my sessions all the time. "I look at the writing credits on a Beyoncé song and see six writers. Do I need a team? How can I hope to be heard if I'm not part of one of these writing crews?" It's a tough one. Keep in mind, not every song is a hit by committee.

**What makes you different
as a songwriter?**

**Two ways to go.** One: Find an artist, look for local talent, and create your own team. If you're a writer but have no aspirations to produce, find someone who is interested in production and work with them. Hit songwriter Liz Rose co-wrote with Taylor Swift when no one really wanted to know about her. Worked out well for Liz.

Two: Join a team. Anything from track builders to vibe masters who know how to get the most out of co-writing with an artist. You gain entry to the writing process, and some who have done this have moved from being the fourth writer on a song to producing artists and co-writing with them. I did this for a few years with Eliot Kennedy and his hit machine Steelworks in the UK. By getting access to the artists he was working with, I got cuts with many of them, including the number one "Day and Night" by Billie Piper.

So much goes into writing a hit. Does luck play a part? There's a loaded question. Kenny Aronoff is not only the most successful session drummer around, but also the most relentless, hardworking musician I know. He did a workshop in which an attendee asked him if he feels he got lucky. He was a little pissed by this. (The term *righteous indignation* comes to mind.) His response was that anybody can get lucky . . . once. Once is not a career. I share the same sentiment about songwriting. It's all about the hard work. I've had some great cuts and a few hits, and like every songwriting friend who's had a few, I would never use the term *lucky*. Even one-hit wonders always have their backstories, and they always involve working for it.

That takes us right to the next stop. What is success for a songwriter?

# CHAPTER 19

# HOW DO YOU MEASURE SUCCESS?

**Come walk with me, darlin', in the cold September rain.**

Plenty of ways.

**Cuts?** That's a biggie. Pro songwriting gets competitive. You need traction to attract a publisher, and you need cuts to keep one. Above all, you need cuts to earn income to actually BE a pro songwriter.

**Awards?** Depends. It's a measure but not one everyone uses or pays attention to. I mentioned earlier my frequent co-writer Kye Fleming is in the Nashville Songwriters Hall of Fame, Writer of the Year three times both in country and pop. Yet I've never seen a single award in her home. I wrote with Graham Lyle years back at his home in England. The Grammy trophy for Song of the Year ("What's Love Got to Do with It") not only was a doorstop to his studio, but it was also broken. As for me, I have a bunch of framed awards on the wall of my studio, always have. What's the difference? Kye felt seeing all that stuff might make her lazy. I like to see the awards to remind myself I've done it before and can do it again. Graham? Don't know; he might have just needed a good doorstop.

**Contests?** I'm a judge for a few of the biggest. The value in competing and winning is that you have some measure of progress compared to all the other entries. Contests are an imperfect process, but it's one any songwriter has access to, and the two takeaways are traction and affirmation. Affirmation is important and can be the very thing you need when things go quiet . . . and they will from time to time.

**Money?** Here's a rocky road. On the one hand, I could consider myself a successful songwriter because I've actually made money from my songs. On the other hand, I've heard songs I would have died to write, but their authors can't make a living. Don't get me wrong, I'm beyond grateful for everything songwriting has given me. But if money was the most important yardstick, I'd be one miserable guy. There are a lot more songwriters with waaaay more cash than me. It can't be the end-all, be-all measurement for success.

And speaking of measurements, don't measure your success by

the Lennons and McCartneys of our world. You're always going to come up short and probably be frustrated for life. Put your songs up against theirs to measure your progress. If you don't feel the need to give up then and there, that's success.

These four are probably the measures most talked about, but the most important one, to my mind, is communication. We all start out writing to communicate something inside.

**I saw Bruce** Springsteen on Broadway, and it was truly awesome. He can communicate like an evangelist—powerful stuff. I went away with something he said in the very first couple of minutes. He described his songwriting as a "magic trick." And it's one awesome two-hour magic trick he pulls off every night.

I don't think it gets any better than that—when you've honed your skill to the point you can move someone. I've worked with some great writers and artists, and it seems to be a common trait: the need to communicate.

If you ask most successful songwriters to name their favorite songs they've written, you're going to hear about songs that never got recorded. Me too. These are the ones in which the writer used their skill to say something that just had to be said. Something that may have had nothing to do with music trends at the time, but they didn't care. They wrote a song that succeeded on a different level. Might have even been therapeutic, for them or someone else. For example . . .

My dad passed away in 1990. He was Irish-born, Glasgow, Scotland-raised, and migrated to America when he was around sixteen years of age. He and my mom met and married in the years before World War II in Westerly, Rhode Island. They lost their firstborn, a baby girl named Eunice and, over time, had four boys. My mom and dad were inseparable. When he passed, I had no way to express my own grief, let alone my thoughts on how my mother must be coping with hers. I didn't know what to say to her, so I wrote a song imagining how she might remember her husband some days. The song is called "September Rain." My publisher loved it and pitched it relentlessly. Artists like Kenny Rogers would put it on hold only to find it didn't make the cut. I didn't care. Not why I wrote it, I guess. Here's the lyric:

Well she lost another memory today
It was gone before she knew it slipped away
And it's days like this that she sits alone and prays
Remembering the cold September Rain
She met him back when time was still young
And before too long they had time on the run
Making promises in a world gone insane
Hand in hand in the cold September Rain
**He said where you wanna run to?**
**I'll take you there**
**Down where the leaves fall in the lane**
**Every day we'll build a memory,**
**Come walk with me, darlin'**
**In the cold September Rain**
So many things conspired to change their world,
There were bills to pay and brand-new baby girls,
Still she never lost the vision in her brain
Making love in the cold September Rain

**CHORUS**
Now the kids have long grown up and moved away

And he's been gone two years to the day
But she swears she can still hear him plain,
Come walk with me, darlin'
In the cold September Rain

**CHORUS**
Well she lost another memory today . . .

**My mom loved it.** So many people have heard it and told me what it's meant to them and then told me their own stories.

I call that songwriting success. I call the rest the music business.

There's so much power in a well-written song. Power to touch, power to teach, power to share, power to reach into someone else's soul and show them something they might not even know was hiding there until they connect with the emotion in a great song.

**I love coaching writers one-on-one. It's MY new normal!
Photo by Eric Brown.**

# CHAPTER 20

# TOPLINERS AND THE NEW NORMAL

**You may or may not** be familiar with this type of songwriter, but you need to be. A topliner is typically a songwriter singing melodies over premade beats. Years ago, mainly in pop music, it referred to the person who wrote the lyric, but times have changed.

I would wager that the majority of pop hits you're hearing start with a beat. The topliner these days might be one of many asked (or hired) to come into the studio and sing melodies or make up lyrics over beats. Many of the best bring an iPhone loaded with titles, lines, rhymes, and anything that might work its way into a hook. The producer might take a piece from this session and a piece from another and build the song. Not the same as two writers in a room creating the words and music, eh? More of a Frankensong. If your piece makes it into the song stew, you may get a partial credit, or you might just be paid like a session singer for the time spent in the studio. A great topliner can command a high studio rate and/or demand credit. In some instances, they may be able to get back anything they contributed that ends up not being used, but that's tricky.

Some of the best topliners (think Sia) are able to channel that inner kid and throw out anything—nonsense words to start, maybe just a simple line to get the vibe going. If this is your path, find ways to practice this. It's easy to find beats online or create them if you can. Just a four- or eight-bar loop will be enough for you to get a feel for this. When you've honed this particular skill, the same rules apply for networking and letting people hear you.

This is a huge part of the changing landscape of songwriting. The lines are blurred even when people try to decide where a song fits. Hip-hop is now pop, country is closer to what pop used to be, EDM (electronic dance music) is big, and rock, at least as of this writing, is barely breathing.

You see more and more songs lately that, due to losing (or settling) a lawsuit are legally required to add the writers of the original source of inspiration or sample. Case in point: "Uptown Funk" now has nine writers listed. I love that song. Can it still be inspired if it took a village to produce it?

All this is a hot topic of debate with songwriters the past few years. I understand the frustration when they feel it's impossible to break into a production team or to write a song that could be pitched to the Beyoncés of the world. It's not impossible, but it is getting pretty rare to see a song written by one writer, not connected in some fashion to the label or production team associated with the record.

I've had major cuts that I wrote on my own, with a co-writer, with two co-writers, and even a few with five. When I've gotten up to more than three, I got confused about who did what, I admit.

Check out the songwriting credits on the Grammy nominees for Best Song in country and pop for 2019.

## Best Country Song

"Break Up in the End," Cole Swindell (Jessie Jo Dillon, Chase McGill, and Jon Nite, songwriters)

"Dear Hate," Maren Morris featuring Vince Gill (Tom Douglas, David Hodges, and Maren Morris, songwriters)

"I Lived It," Blake Shelton (Rhett Akins, Ross Copperman, Ashley Gorley, and Ben Hayslip, songwriters)

"Space Cowboy," Kacey Musgraves (Luke Laird, Shane McAnally, and Kacey Musgraves, songwriters)

"Tequila," Dan + Shay (Nicolle Gaylon, Jordan Reynolds, and Dan Smyers, songwriters)

"When Someone Stops Loving You," Little Big Town (Hillary Lindsey, Chase McGill, and Lori McKenna, songwriters)

## Song of the Year

"All the Stars" (Kendrick Duckworth, Mark Spears, Al Shuckburgh, Anthony Tiffith, and Solana Rowe, songwriters)

"Boo'd Up" (Larrance Dopson, Joelle James, Ella Mai, and Dijon McFarlane, songwriters)

"God's Plan" (Aubrey Graham, Daveon Jackson, Brock Korsan, Ron Latour, Matthew Samuels, and Noah Shebib, songwriters)

"In My Blood" (Teddy Geiger, Scott Harris, Shawn Mendes, and Geoffrey Warburton, songwriters)

"The Joke" (Brandi Carlile, Dave Cobb, Phil Hanseroth, and Tim Hanseroth, songwriters)

"The Middle" (Sarah Aarons, Jordan K. Johnson, Stefan Johnson, Marcus Lomax, Kyle Trewartha, Michael Trewartha, and Anton Zaslavski, songwriters)

"Shallow" (Lady Gaga, Mark Ronson, Anthony Rossomando, and Andrew Wyatt, songwriters)

"This Is America" (Donald Glover and Ludwig Göransson, songwriters)

Whole lotta names, eh?

**I've been hearing** more and more about artificial intelligence songwriting, using AI to create patterns, random wordings, and more. Most digital audio workstations, such as Logic for instance, can already generate drumbeats and chord changes. Can an AI-generated hit single be far behind? I love technology, and I'm interested to see how this will work for music in the future. I do hope it's more of a production flavor than a song creator.

Another recent development has been giving the songwriter an artist credit. Some of the biggest songwriters in pop are showing up alongside the artist on current hits. This takes some serious leverage on the songwriter side, but if you were providing the songs for artists who have massive hits, you just might be able to get a credit on the master. That's a whole other additional income stream. Producers, especially in rap and hip-hop, have been tapping this extra income source for years. Kind of interesting in that artists have demanded publishing on songs they had no part in writing for years. This could turn the tables in favor of the hit songwriter.

With streaming now equaling two-thirds of the money made from recorded music, we're a far cry from the old model.

In his recent article for *Rolling Stone* magazine, Tim Ingham writes:

> **By the time you finish reading this sentence, three new songs will have been uploaded onto Spotify. This time tomorrow, the number will have risen above 20,000 songs—a daily deluge of music which would take you a month and a half to listen to . . . without sleep. By this time next year, more than 7 million new tracks will have been crammed onto the service.**

Spotify boss Daniel Ek revealed these numbers back in March at his company's Investor Day in New York, and the music business hasn't stopped talking about them since. This trend isn't limited to Spotify either. On other music-streaming services, it's even worse: the CEO of Rhapsody and Napster, Bill Patrizio, confirmed in June that his platform ingests 24,000 new tracks each day, or 1,000 tracks per hour. Anyone else starting to feel a bit overwhelmed?

In the end, this current state is just that—the current state. Complaining about the songwriting business and how unfair it is or how "watered down" the songs are is good fodder for social media posts but not for change. It's an ever-evolving business. Finding where you belong as a songwriter is more important than ever. However you choose to write songs, be awesome and the road gets easier.

**Complaining about the songwriting business and how unfair it is or how "watered down" the songs are is good fodder for social media posts but not for change.**

# PART 3

# THE PAYOFF

**Meeting up with a musical hero. (L to R) Our daughters, Morgan and Taylor, Sting, Kye Fleming, me, Kipper, and Kathy.**

# CHAPTER 21

# MENTORS, HEROES, AND TOOLS

I never had a mentor. I had great parents, supportive to the point of opening their home (and fridge) to all of my musician friends. Hazel, my mom, would drive her underage son to his club gigs in upper New York state, usually towing the keyboard player's Hammond B3. She would sit in the car for four hours, reading a book by flashlight, then drive me home afterward.

**But I had no one** who had any experience in the field I was plowing. I would have given anything to have been able to pick the brain of a songwriter. This is one of the reasons I love coaching writers. I can take every hard-earned lesson and pass it on. Wisdom.

You can find wisdom in so many places now: books about songwriting, YouTube videos, movies, songwriting organizations, workshops and retreats, even online one-on-one coaching. It's all out there, but it's all only information until you turn it into inspiration.

Always consider the source when you're on this wisdom mission.

When I look at a songwriting book, I turn it over to see if the person sharing their knowledge has actually done what I want to do. I have to feel I'm getting expertise from an expert. I distrust someone telling me how to do something they haven't done and done really well themselves. As with most things, there are exceptions—in this case, the people who have immersed themselves in the craft, deconstructed, dissected, interviewed, and interrogated great songs and great writers to be able to develop a course or a method to help you.

I do have heroes. I got some of my most valuable songwriting tools by reading their autobiographies, from Cole Porter and Irving Berlin to the pioneers of rock and roll, from the Beatles to Charlie Parker, Bob Dylan, Stephen Sondheim, and Andrew Lloyd Webber. I've also picked up some great creative habits from reading about Picasso, Michelangelo, Twyla Tharp, Maya Angelou, Marlon Brando, and Richard Pryor. Reading about how they did what they did contributed to my songwriting DNA. When people excel and tell you how they did it, you're bound to find tools you can implement.

I've heard people say they don't want to meet their heroes for fear of being let down. Whenever I've met artists I admire, they have been gracious to a fault. It's the ones who are the imposters that have given me grief. True artists can be insecure as people, but not when it comes to their art. I'm talking about the ones who have stuck around. When I was in Faith Band with a record deal and sharing stages with artists such as the Allman Brothers, Fleetwood Mac, the Doobie Brothers, Thin Lizzy, and Hall & Oates, they (and their crews) treated us like equals. They knew the road we were on and the odds we faced, and they were quick to make it as easy on us as possible. Lots of the one-hit wonders we opened for made our world miserable—as miserable as theirs probably was on the way back down.

If you should find yourself face-to-face with your hero, just be you. It's a slightly awkward position for you both, and later you'll probably think of everything you wish you had said. But just being yourself is the only way I know of not to make a mess of it.

When I was introduced to Sting, whose songwriting I love, I stood there for a few long minutes saying things like, "So how are you liking Nashville?" and "Isn't Kipper [who had introduced us] awesome?" I had similar experiences with Barbra Streisand and even Tiny Tim, although Tiny was pretty talkative. His manager pulled me aside to say, "Please don't let Tim make a phone call." Evidently, Tiny would call for a pizza delivery whenever he had the chance, and he had kind of blown up from his heyday. I guess Big Tim was not an option.

I ran into Felix Cavaliere in a bookstore. I had grown up with the Young Rascals, and his organ solo in "Good Lovin'" has to be one of rock's finest moments. This conversation went much better, as I started by just thanking him for the music and memories. That opened up a lovely conversation that included his asking me about my music and saying he "has heard of me." Might have just been being kind, but I'll choose to believe.

One of the more surreal star hangs had to be with Cher at Miles Copeland's third castle retreat in the South of France. When I woke up and went down for coffee to find Cher at the table, talking over breakfast, all I could think of was the old *Sonny & Cher* show. A few of us even went into the closest town to browse; watching people realize that was Cher walking around their little village was fun. She was great, very down to earth, and easy to talk to.

I hope you're finding your heroes and mentors. These are the good people, the valuable tools you need on this road. Let me introduce you to a different kind of songwriting tool. If you haven't met him yet, you probably will. Most songwriters I coach know him well.

**I'm talking about** That Guy. The one who's learned just enough to be dangerous and just enough to hold it over you in a co-write or a conversation. You know the saying, "A little knowledge is a dangerous thing"? That's The Guy. He's learned just enough tools to become one.

From the *Urban Dictionary* definition:

> *Tool: (noun) Someone whose ego FAR exceeds his talent, intelligence, and likeability. But, of course, he is clueless regarding that fact. He erroneously thinks he is THE MAN!*

Usually, That Guy has taken useful tools and turned them into his own rules for songwriting. Maybe you've put that great idea out there in your co-write, and he tells you too many reasons why that's just not done. I've talked to writers who have been close to tears after working with That Guy who go away thinking they have no business writing since they don't seem to follow the gospel according to That Guy.

There is no one way to write. If there are any rules, well, there aren't any that can't be bent or broken. And that's where tools over rules comes in. In the wrong hands, the best tools become a lethal weapon.

When I was growing up, my dad and brothers could build any-thing. They were amazing with tools and always seemed to know the right ones to use. Me? Not so much. The same tool in my un-skilled hands was just an instrument of destruction. To this day, if my wife (who is great with tools) sees me pick up a hammer, she'll say, "Here, let me help you with that," and take it away from me.

So what can you do? If you're in a co-write, on a social media board, or wherever you find That Guy, just shine him on. Don't be intimidated. Follow your path, seek out the best tools from a master craftsman, and use them. Just don't become one!

Keep looking for those who can inspire you. Maybe you can reach back and help other songwriters. You might feel like you aren't in that position yet, but I bet there is something you can do. I love it when I see songwriters, not necessarily the famous ones but the ones who are learning their craft, sharing it in hospitals, music therapy, summer camps, schools, or by playing in nursing homes. Sharing this gift and passion you have will pay you back tenfold and believe me, the people you meet won't care if you're a name or a nobody.

**When people excel and tell you how they did it, you're bound to find tools you can implement.**

**Me and the muse go missing!**

## CHAPTER 22

# WHEN THE MUSE GOES MISSING

You've been there. I've been there. Every songwriter I know has been there. It's an occupational hazard. You can call it brain dead, blank page-itis, or by its more common name, writer's block. It is the dreaded state of "I got nothin'."

The muse has gone missing.

**It sucks**. You sit down to write, you have the time, you have the will, you have the tools and . . . nothing. Nothing for hours, nothing for days. You beat yourself up, and the critic takes center stage. "How did you ever come up with anything in the first place?" "What makes you think someone will actually want to record your song?" "You call yourself a songwriter . . . really?"

If you're totally dependent on inspiration in the form of a muse, you're already in trouble. You may be inspired sometimes and come up with something that feels almost like you were guided, but the truth is, if you plan to do this as a career, you can't depend on the muse being around 24-7.

So what do you do? You prepare. You prepare for the times that you want to write but don't feel that divine inspiration. I've picked up tons of tips from writers and artists I've worked with about this subject and ways to deal with it. Remember the ideas I talked about in chapter 2?

- Deciding to be intentional in your search for lines and titles?
- Things that could make their way into your writing at a later date? Wandering down bookstore aisles, watching TV and movies with a pad and a pen, waiting for that one great line?
- Recording the smallest of ideas, snippets of melodies, conversations, anything that might take the place of the muse for a day and get you writing?

Thinking of your path as a writer's *life* instead of a day at a time, more like a marathon than a sprint, can ease the pressure of a bad writing day. It's hard enough looking at a blank piece of paper, but if you're waiting on your muse to show up to get you going, it can be a loooooong day.

Try using some tools I've mentioned to get you unstuck:

- Switch instruments.
- Try creating your melody away from your instrument.
- Deconstruct songs you love.
- Spend a day just listening, immersing yourself in one artist.

Once you decide these types of tools are every bit as valuable as the days in front of your computer, keyboard, or guitar, it actually starts to be freeing. Less pressure.

There is a story about Winston Churchill and his love of painting. The old boy got pretty good at it later in life but always had trouble tuning out and getting started. Sure, he didn't have the internet and only had the pesky World War II thing to distract him, but he found a simple way to push the voices down: he just threw some paint against the canvas. Once he did that, he was in.

There's also nothing wrong with putting your tools away for a while, just stopping. I have a room full of guitars but have gone weeks without picking one up if I know I'm not really ready to commit. Might just be me, but I feel it's almost a sacred thing when you pick up an instrument or sit at a desk or keyboard with the intent of writing a song. I want to give the process the respect it deserves. I understand you may have a deadline from time to time, and I actually love deadlines as a songwriter, but there will be times when it's a blood-from-a-stone thing.

Reading is another tool to stave off your own blank page. Read anything and everything. There's inspiration in every dog-eared book I've ever owned. Maybe you're in a hunting-and-gathering season as a songwriter. Store it up for later.

Exercise is a great unblocking tool. When your body is busy doing something physical, your mind can be free to roam. Loads of life-long songwriters go for a drive. I'm not suggesting you drive and write at the same time, but keeping something close by to record with has been a go-to for me. Both sides of the brain are working while you're doing something physical.

Finding ways to break up the routine of writing can get you back on track. Traveling may be my favorite. Most writing trips I've been on have involved getting to a city a day or two early and staying a day or two after, just to soak it in. I trust that it's going to be an intake of inspiration. Might resurface down the line or the day of a write, but I'm filling the well.

**Ever heard the phrase**, "What's down in the well comes up in the bucket"? You can think of writer's block as a well running dry, which suggests how to stay ahead of writer's block. When I've felt worn out from coming up with ideas, I remind myself that my well is either close to empty or I'm filling it with the wrong things. "Garbage in, garbage out," to quote a more colorful phrase. If I'm spending my time watching junk or finding diversions to keep from writing, that's the very stuff that's going directly into my well. Easy to do—when writing gets hard, I can justify a bunch of guilty pleasures. The trouble is, those guilty pleasures usually don't help with that bucket thing.

I look for the things that require extra focus. Miles Davis, TED Talks, biographies, podcasts, conversations . . . anything that has a chance of bringing my subconscious into play. I'm a big believer in the subconscious acting like a great co-writer. Your subconscious wants to be challenged to solve problems or to connect the dots. I can imagine it looking at the contents of my bucket sometimes and asking, "Is this all ya got?" So I try to feed it. It's our job as creatives to constantly fill the well with the good stuff so that when the bucket comes up, we're inspired and ready to write.

It helps to remember you're a songwriter even while you're doing other things. Get away from your songwriting routine when you're feeling that fear of the blank page. Just because you're not trying to write a song today doesn't mean you won't tomorrow. You've written a song before; you'll write another one. It's sometimes hard to believe the world is not waiting on you or me to write one today, but it's true. So step away, refresh, fill the well, and dip the bucket in when you're ready.

Sometimes it's as simple as taking a rest. I heard about a writer who had written a massive country hit and attributed the song to a dream he had. He began taking afternoon naps. When his wife asked him to nap less and spend a little more time on the honey-do-list, he replied, "I'm not just sleeping; I'm working." Nice work if you can get it.

**"**

**Prepare for the times that you want to write but don't feel that divine inspiration.**

**"**

# CHAPTER 23

# WHEN THE MUSE SHOWS UP

**She's back and he's happy!**

When coaching songwriters, I ask them to focus on tools. If they're going to write for years, they can't wait for lightning to hit them. For every story about Sir Paul dreaming "Yesterday" as "Scrambled Eggs" or Keith recording the riff to "Satisfaction" and then going back to sleep, there are so many more stories about the craft, about applying everything you know to help an idea unfold. Sort of the "constant gardener" route.

**I believe this**, although I never want to discourage a writer from just "receiving" because sometimes you do get handed that gift. The muse shows up. Most hit songwriters will tell you that anybody can have the idea, but it's knowing how to actually form it and develop it that's the difference between the muse showing up and actually writing the song. That's craft.

As for the muse, she is almost always a she. Fine by me. If you're working at this, your antenna is up. Those ideas are out there, but you have to be willing and able to not only grab them but also form them. I'm betting you've had this experience a few times by now. The muse made an appearance, and the song was effortless. If it works once, it can get contagious or even addictive. You can find yourself standing outside with a lightning rod, manning a Ouija board, conducting a song séance, or standing over Elvis's grave. Done that once. Twice. Nothing.

You can't summon the muse. She shows up when she shows up. All you can do is recognize her, drop everything, and take it as far as you can. I've written songs like that more than once. You feel it, you write nonstop, drop your pen, and sit back amazed.

In 2017, I met my friend John Hartley at the Frothy Monkey in Franklin, Tennessee. John is a very well-known and beloved Christian writer, producer, and record executive. I am a Christian (an ex-Catholic, which explains a lot if you know our type) but not much of a contemporary Christian music fan. Nothing against the form, but it just doesn't move me like the old hymns and spirituals. John and I bonded when we first met, not over Christian music but our love of '70s and '80s Brit pop.

John has offered me entrée to the best songwriters in the Christian praise and worship field. Tempting to co-write—it's maybe the most lucrative field for songwriters at the moment—but I've always said no. I won't write it like the writers who live and breathe it, so it's bound to be less than great in my mind.

On this day, John opened with, "I know you don't want to write praise and worship songs, but you've told me how much you love

the old church standards, right? Ever heard of Fanny Crosby?"
Fanny Crosby is the most recorded songwriter of praise and worship in history. She wrote so many cuts that she had to develop
pseudonyms because people simply didn't want any more Fanny
songs. Yep, I knew who Fanny was all right.

The queen of Gospel songwriters. Most hymnals have a few of
her classic songs such as "Blessed Assurance," "Jesus Is Tenderly
Calling You Home," and "To God Be the Glory." Born in 1820 and
died in 1915. She was also blind since early childhood.

John had been put in charge of creating a project to match a cache
of never-before-seen lyrics from Fanny's estate. The idea was to
give a few songwriters a certain number of the lyrics and let them
write melodies. Basically, write a song using her lyrics. They would
then pick artists to record the songs for a few planned albums.

This was iconic stuff. I protested for a minute: "I've never written
a hymn," "Not my thing," "Wouldn't know where to start." To
which John just said he didn't want me to try and write a hymn,
just write what I feel. I ran out of ways to say no. A few weeks
later, I received about fifteen lyrics transcribed from the originals,
which by all accounts were hard to read. I picked five.

**This was so unique** to me that I didn't want to treat it like anything I'd ever done. Not even sure why, but it felt right to spread
the lyrics out on the desk in my studio and *not* try to write them
for a while. I would go by and scan them some days, but I was
determined not to write them in any way I was used to.

One day, I picked up my Telecaster, plugged it into a Vox A30,
started playing some chord changes followed by a melody, walked

over to a lyric called "Love Divine," and just sang it. From start to finish. It felt like something I'd heard before, something familiar. But it wasn't. It was a complete, new song. A Crosby and Cawley song.

It almost scared the crap out of me the way it happened. And then it happened again a few days later with another one, and a few weeks later with a third. I've never had a songwriting experience like that. It was a muse, maybe, but I felt I'd been gifted those melodies. Not sure how they will be used, but John and I did get together to write a Christmas song from another of Fanny's lyrics called "Find Him in a Manger" that appeared on the album *The Best of Christmas in America* on the Public Square Volume One. Planning on writing more with John in the future and hoping the muse makes a return appearance.

You can't base a *career* in songwriting on pure inspiration. You need tools to come up with songs when you don't have that lightning-in-a-bottle thing. But you do this long enough and the muse will show up. You just need to know what to do with her when she does.

**It almost scared the crap out of
me the way it happened.**

**A country hit with a UK legend, Lulu, at our home in Kingston Springs, Tennessee, 1997.**

# CHAPTER 24

# THRIVING AND SURVIVING

If you've been writing songs for any amount of time, you know by now you're going to subject yourself to some of the highest highs and lowest lows imaginable. We're not talking life and death here, but if dreams have a life, then maybe we are.

You may already be at the point where your songs are being heard by the people who can actually make some of those dreams come true, or maybe you're doing it yourself: playing live, making records. Either way, you dream big. You wouldn't have it any other way. The idea that something could start in your head and make its way to someone's heart, create memories, help, heal, or just take them away for a while is the stuff I'm talking about.

It's the kind of thing family and friends might think is cute while you're waiting for your real life. But you know better. It's the most real thing in your life. You need to write to breathe.

**When every star aligns**, your song gets cut, and other people actually get to hear what you hear, it's the most surreal and amazing moment outside of the birth of a child. It's a big, big life, and you can be forgiven for wanting everyone to feel what you feel. I've been blessed to have a few of those moments.

And if you've been doing this long enough at that level, there can be another part of life that comes in uninvited: death—death of an idea, a hope, or a dream. And it hurts. Feels like you flew too close to the sun. Sound dramatic? Maybe to those friends and family but, again you know better.

You don't find a way to "get over it"; you learn what you have to do to "get on with it." Some writers never do. They're the ones who tell you how the business sucks, how unfair, fixed, broken, and backward-thinking all the players in it are. If you reach that point, the well hasn't just run dry; it's become poisoned.

Those feelings always scared me to death. Anything but that. Lord knows it's hard enough to succeed in the arts, but without the ability to dream? Impossible. You never get used to disappointment, but knowing it when you meet it and knowing how to deal with it are great tools for a songwriter.

I want to share one of the most trying times of my life, not just as a songwriter but also as a husband and a father making his living in this business.

My introduction to Wynonna Judd was a phone call from the legendary producer and label head Tony Brown, sometime around late 1991. This was one of those dream calls for a songwriter. She had heard some of my songs, and while in a meeting with Tony, they tracked me down at home. Tony put Wynonna on the phone; she asked if I could send anything and everything I had ASAP.

This was the start of a long and winding road and, like most things in music, didn't go quite as smoothly as I planned.

She didn't use anything of mine for her first solo record, *Wynonna*, but I did come down and meet her in Nashville, thanks to my buddy John Cooper, who was mixing her concerts at the time. Her voice blew me away and still does.

Flash forward to 1995–96. She had cut a song I had written with Kye Fleming and Mary Ann Kennedy called "Can't Stop My Heart" for her third album, *Revelations*. We were all huge fans, and the song was perfect for her. I had just moved to Nashville with my wife, Kathy, and two young daughters, Taylor and Morgan. We had bought a house and were busy having my dream studio built on to it. I had also just signed the most lucrative contract I'd ever had with Windswept Pacific Music. I was really counting on this cut to kick things into high gear. I literally banked on it.

One day, we got a call that they were in the studio going over the song again and felt they hadn't quite captured the feel of the original demo. They had a couple of questions. I explained it was a drum loop, an eight-bar drum pattern that repeated—not all that common at the time in Nashville. But I figured it's Nashville, best players in the world, they'll nail it eventually. But "Can't Stop My Heart" just about did; they dropped it.

I was stunned. I thought the stars had aligned with this one: I had written it with two of my best friends; an artist I loved was recording it. This seemed like a perfect single on an album every writer in town wanted on. Every songwriter has the ones that got away and I'd had my share, including a song I wrote for one of my heroes, Roy Orbison. He cut it for his *Mystery Girl* album but passed away before doing a vocal. Still, this one was different somehow.

One of the most heartbreaking moments in my life to this day was when I sat down with Kathy and explained what had happened. Until then, I had been supremely confident that my talent and drive were going to collide with our dreams and change our lives. My wife had put all her trust in a dreamer, and at that moment, I felt a fool. I don't remember if I even looked her in the eyes during that nightmare conversation. All I could say was I was sorry.

Now, Kathy is a strong woman of faith, and faith can be contagious. We worked through it. We were bruised but not beaten. We prayed for our family, our decisions, she told me she had faith in me, and we vowed to move on.

**Here's where the faith** part got pretty interesting. A few weeks passed, and I get a call from John Cooper, still working for Wynonna and now my neighbor in Kingston Springs, Tennessee. "Too bad about 'Can't Stop My Heart,'" he said. "At least the other one is still on the record." *The other one?*

Turns out Wynonna had cut a song I'd written with Lulu and her brother Billy Lawrie in England. It wasn't remotely country, I didn't even know she'd heard it, and no one told us they were even thinking about cutting it. "My Angel Is Here" made it onto *Revelations.*

The album entered the charts in '96 at number two and stayed there a long time (stuck behind Shania Twain) on the pop and country charts. It went platinum—the song even came out as the third single but didn't fare too well. I didn't really mind, because I felt like I'd been thrown a lifeline. One of the highlights was going to the taping for her TV special *Wynonna: Revelations* (1996) and having her stop the taping to say hi to me, Kathy, and our daughters. "My Angel Is Here" didn't do that well as a single, but the amazing thing to me was the B side, "Change the World." Eric Clapton later cut it, and it won a Grammy for song of the year—the girl can pick 'em.

**❝**

**You don't find a way to "get over it"; you learn what you have to do to "get on with it."**

**❞**

**We all need somebody to navigate the ups and downs.
My wife, Kathy. Photo by Tiffany Dupree.**

# CHAPTER 25

# CELEBRATING AND GRIEVING

Kathy asked me years ago why I had awards and records on the wall my studio. I thought hard about it. Does my ego need constant feeding? I hope not. In the end, what I love about seeing them is that I can be reassured that this thing I'm trying to do— conjure up a song on any given day—really can work. Proof.

Where does your affirmation come from? When you write songs, it's hard to come by but so important. Songwriting is a solitary journey so much of the time. Hard to tell if you're on course or hopelessly lost.

Here are a few things to do.

Celebrate the victories, big and small, and remember to affirm yourself from time to time, in whatever form that takes. We all need it, and most of the time, it's going to have to come from within. Take time to celebrate your hard work, and remember to praise someone else's when you get the chance.

What does that look like? Take yourself to lunch. Treat yourself to something you've been eyeballing. Not talking going out and getting a new ride here—more like a pair of shoes. Whatever it is for you that allows you to reflect and rejoice. You've been digging in, studying your craft, when all of a sudden you see a ray of light. It's making sense. Make no mistake, these are little victories, and you need to celebrate them from time to time. Maybe no one else understands the reason for the victory dance, but that's OK. If you have family, friends close by, include them. They may not know what you've had to do to get to the party, but they'll be happy for you and that glow can carry you through the dark days.

**Take time to celebrate your hard work and remember to praise someone else's when you get the chance.**

**Some writers love** to journal. It's a terrific tool but not one I've ever stuck with. I admire writers who can, because they can look back and see those victories. They're in the pages.

Writing a song never gets any better than the day you finish and can stand back and admire it. A magic trick all right, and you pulled it off. Pulled it out of thin air. There was nothing there yesterday and now . . . voilà, a song. Now's not the time to hold it up against the competition or to measure it by any standard other than your own. You did it. From your mind to the world.

Throw yourself a party. Then get back on the ride.

So much of what we do as writers is impossible to measure. As weird as it seems, I always loved mowing the lawn. I could start the job, do it well, and actually see it completed. There it was, job done. Maybe you have your own version of landscaping. It's important not to feel that everything in your life is floating and waiting to be completed. Sometimes it's hard to tell when that moment is.

Just as important as celebrating your victories is knowing how to grieve. Maybe you've put your heart and soul into a song, you love it, it checks all the boxes for you. You sent it in for a critique, and deep down you're prepping for that "wow!" You get "nice." Nice is a kiss on the cheek. Nice is not wow. Nice is "well done." Nice is "good." Good is the enemy of great.

**Just as important as celebrating your victories is knowing how to grieve.**

**Truth be told,** you're going to have way more of these scenarios than the one you envisioned, especially in the early days of getting your songs from the bedroom to the boardroom. It's what you do now that can shape you as a writer. How do you handle criticism or that big break that just broke down?

Grieve. Grieve for a specific amount of time. Let everyone around you know you're grieving. Let them know it's nothing personal, nothing they did; it's just something you have to do. No matter how well things were going, it still hurt when I lost a cut. Rather than freaking out with no end in sight, I found a method that worked for me. I would acknowledge that I had lost something I cared deeply about, told the people close to me what was up, tried to keep to myself, and just grieved. I wasn't fun to be around. My process might have involved too much wine, tossing a few things around my studio, cussing the powers that be and railing against the songwriting gods . . . for two days. After that, I was expected to be a human being again and reenter polite society.

Once I gave myself permission to grieve, it got easier to ride out the storms. I like to think I've mellowed out and can handle defeat better. One gift of getting older is you really can look back and realize it wasn't life and death.

At one juncture a few years ago, the business had just beaten me senseless. Nothing I was doing was bringing the result I had come to expect. This grieving session went on far too long. Kathy finally told me I was going to get off my butt, get out of my own head, get out of the house, drive into town, and volunteer. As far from my comfort zone as I'd ever been. I picked GraceWorks in Franklin, Tennessee. GraceWorks provides financial relief as well as food and clothing to the people in need in our community. I worked as a counselor every Wednesday after that for four years and even ended up on the board of directors. Best thing I ever did to get over myself and my grief.

Maybe a trip works for you. Getting away from your songwriting for a spell. Maybe you even pamper your poor, poor self for a day or two. I can't recommend the red wine route, but whatever works to get you past the bad news and back on track is for you to figure out and practice. Nobody outside your loved ones really wants to hear your "one that got away" story if it's tinged with bitterness. Maybe the price we have to pay to dream big is to fall hard once in a while. Maybe we're meant to suffer to know the difference. Not my call.

I have a friend who has a great saying for when the chaos is out of their control: "Not my circus, not my monkeys." Works for me.

# CHAPTER 26

# POWER UP

**Knowledge is power, and you can't start too early.
I loved teaching these high school kids at Jam Camp.
Endsworth High School, Nashville.**

**I'll say it again:** knowledge is power, and it's easier than ever to get. But for whatever reason, most songwriters (myself included in the early years) put all their energy into the creative process and view the business as a necessary evil or something that will take care of itself.

·The following ten statements are things I've heard from prospective coaching clients that go a long way to illustrating my point of needing to understand the world you're in to function well.

*I'm hoping to sell my songs.*

- You don't "sell" songs. You hope to get them published and keep the writer's share at the very least. Fight for your publishing rights.

*Someone offered to demo my song for $2,500 and get it to some people in the business.*

- Run—fast.

*I'm looking for a $75,000–$100,000 job as a staff writer. Will relocate to Nashville if I need to.*

- Me too! Doesn't exist these days. Deals are just different.

*My songs are better than 99 percent of the crap on the radio.*

- Really? You're still writing for a listener in the end, the person in the car. Find out how to reach them.

*I don't believe in rewriting. Either the muse brings an idea fully developed, or it's not worth it.*

- How many songs have you written? How many have been cut? Rewriting is hard, but it's one thing that can separate the wannabes from the pros.

*You can't teach writing, but I'm willing to give you a shot.* (I love this one.)

- I disagree, but I understand the point. You can give someone tools and expertise. What they do with it is the deal. Information into inspiration.

*I don't know why I haven't received any royalties on the CD that I sell at my shows.*

- Google ASCAP, BMI, and SESAC and find out how money is made from songwriting. If you aren't registered with one of those, you won't be making any money from songwriting. Understand performance and mechanical royalties, self-publishing, Harry Fox, and more.

*I'm only interested in co-writing if I can "write up."*

- Get really good at what you do. Network, play nice, and hope you get the shot to show what you can do. Pray that "write up" writer needs a boost from what you got.

*Networking is for nerds; the song should speak for itself.*

- The song can't speak for itself if no one hears it.

*Music, intellectual property, and expertise should be free.*

- Do you go to your doctor for free? Do you hire plumbers and electricians for free? Get your car repaired for free? Cable? Entertainment? Of course you don't. Why on earth should music and something that someone's created through their hard work and expertise be free?

Don't get me wrong, I'm not knocking the statements or questions I get from writers. I just don't want them (or you) to be uninformed when the information is out there. I learned so much of what I know about songwriting the hard way; you don't have to.

Knowing your strength as a songwriter is vital. Even if you only write on your own, knowing the areas where you need to bulk up is a must. If you're co-writing or looking to, be honest with yourself when you seek out co-writers. If you tend to be more comfortable writing melodies, then by all means look for a strong lyricist. I know it may seem like common sense, but we can all be guilty of thinking "because we can do everything, we should do everything." I have been in plenty of co-writes when someone in the room insisted on getting their lyric input in the song when in truth another writer was waaaay more qualified to come up with a killer line. It's a sign of a mature writer when they can focus on what they do best and let the other writer do the same. At the end of the day, it's all about the listener. They don't care who did what; they care if it's a song they can love. I've gone into a co-write with guns blazing. It never worked out well. I learned to be prepared but ready to listen to what the other writer had to say.

If you know your strengths, it doesn't mean you have to abandon your weaknesses. Just work on your weaknesses to make them strengths. Build them up while you lead with your strong suit. You never stop learning on this journey no matter how many writing situations you end up in or how many songs you birth. You've probably heard songwriters say that it's a muscle. You have to use it, or it will atrophy. I agree, but this can be tough if you think the only way to exercise it is to sit down and write. Everything you can do to add to your path will keep that muscle pumping, and that includes using YouTube for songwriting talks, seminars, free guitar lessons, and theory instructors. There are also industry blogs, behind-the-scenes books by top artists, mentors, tutors, and coaches.

**Not everything is free**, but it is available. You can study Bob Dylan's lyrics, watch someone dissect a Beatles song, listen in to John Mayer talking to students at Berklee, send your lyric to be critiqued by a pro, even pay for one-on-one mentoring from someone who's actually done what you aspire to do. When I started out, I didn't even know you could have a *career* as a writer. I didn't know a songwriter and no one I knew had ever met one.

Even if I'd had the money, which I never did, there was no one to pay to teach me. Different world. I couldn't even ask the questions. Now the answers are out there for you to find, so there's no excuse for not being a powerful songwriter.

**"**

**At the end of the day,
it's all about the listener.**

**"**

# CHAPTER 27

# BECOMING A FEARLESS SONGWRITER

**Not exactly fearless here in the early '70s! My first big-time session at the Hit Factory, New York City.**

I've introduced you to two of my "Holy Trinity" of favorite co-writers, Kye Fleming and Brenda Russell. I've learned a bunch from each one, each one is a lifelong, trusted friend, and each one is a fearless songwriter. Being fearless is one of the best traits a songwriter can have.

Eliot Kennedy is the third. A six-foot six-inch gentle giant of a guy from Sheffield, England. El is self-taught, can play most everything well, is a businessman, vibe master, great producer, and a fearless creator. Just like Kye and Brenda, Eliot and I share a wicked sense of humor, a love of many things outside of music, and an ability to instantly turn into six-year-olds. Six-year-olds are generally fearless when it comes to art. Give them a canvas and some colors, and they'll use them all. They aren't waiting for a critique or approval, nor are they worried about how commercial or acceptable their work of art might be. They just go for it.

**My favorite people** to work with are like that, and I hope I am, too—may not always nail it but not afraid to play the fool once in a while. Each of us has tackled areas way outside of our songwriting comfort zone and we all know the value of that. Eliot and Brenda have written music for Broadway—*Finding Neverland* and *The Color Purple*, respectively. Kye has illustrated children's books. I'm coaching and writing a book here. None of us had any background in these endeavors. We do them because we don't see why we can't.

I don't want to compare these feats to people who are truly fearless: firefighters, pilots, policemen, surgeons—these people *have* to be fearless. In our songwriting world and in our own way, we've learned to trust the idea of walking the wire without a net, which might have started with the idea of "no plan B." Kye and I were interviewed at a West Coast Songwriters Association event once and asked about our plan Bs. We replied in unison, "What plan B?" If you have a plan B, you have a backup plan to fail. You need to put your whole heart into writing songs. Anything less and you're going to be second to the writer who does.

This thing we do is not a thing you can study and know right away if you're going to succeed. I coach a few lawyers, a couple of doctors—including a brain surgeon in Boston—a concert pianist, and even a guy in the UK who manages a large hospital. They all share a trait. They excel at what they were trained to do. I admire them because they really want to write songs, but a stumbling block can be the fact that their career path has been more measurable. Songwriting is harder to measure. Sure, you learn your craft, you learn some rules . . . and then you break them. Ever see works by Picasso when he was a student? I saw an exhibit in Barcelona of his early work. Could have been anybody. But he was learning the rules before he blew them up. Betting old Pablo didn't have a plan B, but I do know he was fearless. Who puts one eye in the middle of a head?

I mentioned early in the book about getting together with Kye and Brenda in Nashville to write "Dancing in My Dreams." To this day, that was my favorite co-writing experience ever. By starting out saying we were not going to pay attention to any expectations but our own, we were free, about as far away from a plan B as we could get. We were going to soar or crash and burn; either way, we were going to be fearless. We were. It worked. We learned, and the results followed.

**When we finished** the song, we all knew it. We all were in tears. It was as good as songwriting gets, my friends. Brenda and I ran and demoed it just to be able to play it for ourselves nonstop. Then came the sending-it-to-our-publishers part. Each of our publishers loved it but, like us, really didn't see an obvious home for it.

Brenda's publisher decided it was perfect for Tina Turner. Tina was at the height of her long career, and we'd all been close in the past to landing songs but no cigar. Record label A&R folks generally have a brief that they send out when they are looking for songs for an artist. This song ticked exactly zero boxes for Tina. This publisher's team member who sent it had a gut feeling Tina would love it if she could only hear it. God bless this person.

She sent it in. The story I heard was the label called to ream out the publisher. "This is so far from what we asked for. You should fire the person who wasted our time." They did.

She persisted anyway until Tina finally heard it. That song was the touchstone for an album that went on to sell six million. The moral? Really great artists don't want to repeat themselves. They want to move forward. Most record label people want to replicate success and keep their jobs. The whole process can be fear driven. The true artist? Fearless. The fired girl? Fearless. And you should be, too.

This thinking is why I haven't tried to give you a method. Instead, I've given you tools I've picked up along the way. These are the things that have helped me, and I'm hoping they help you to write the best songs you possibly can.

Once you've had time to try these tools, add yourself to the mix. What makes you unique is going to be the key to your path as a songwriter. Use the information you gather, turn it into inspiration, and be a fearless songwriter.

**You need to put your whole heart into writing songs. Anything less and you're going to be second to the writer who does.**

# CHAPTER 28

# BEST AND WORST ADVICE

**The Richard Avedon cover for the first Faith Band album. High above the Sunset Strip getting ready to fall hard. See point #3 under Worst Advice.**

This is delicate stuff for me. I coach writers all over the world with wildly different goals, talents, and dreams. For me, it's not so much nuts and bolts as trying hard to find real-life examples of a successful path and balancing those with cautionary tales.

**As with any advice,** I start with considering the source. Is the person qualified to give direction? Just by virtue of doing what I do, as long as I've done it, I've built up quite a stash of hard-earned wisdom with plenty of mistakes mixed in. In some of my answers, I may be restating points I've made earlier in the book, but I do so because they deserve to be repeated.

I get asked to write articles for different publications and groups such as *Songwriter Magazine UK*, the USA Songwriting Competition, West Coast Songwriters, *M Magazine*, and the Australian Songwriters Association, to name-drop a few. One asked me to write an article about the best and worst advice I've ever received as a songwriter. Here's some of what I came up with.

## THE WORST ADVICE

1. **Have a plan B.** To do this job, you have to not be able to not write.
2. **Only write what you know.** You can argue this, as I have with several of my coaching clients. "The only true songs are the songs written from my own personal experience." That's the argument. I would argue that unless your life is unbelievably interesting and eventful, the well will run dry quickly. It's great to write from real life, but it's also pretty cool to make something up sometimes.
3. **Focus only on being creative. Someone else will do that messy "business" part.** I tried that; doesn't work. Be a student of the business. I've said this many times already, but it is important and bears repeating: it's your career, and no one is going to care about your career like you do.
4. **Follow the songwriting rules.** Obviously, learn 'em so you can break 'em. Like any craft, you want to learn the ABCs . . . but then you want to invent some of your own.

**Great art requires suffering.** I've written some of my best sad songs when I was insanely happy and some of the most upbeat ones when I was down. If you just write every day, you'll experience it all.

## THE BEST ADVICE

1. **Jump.** When you're stuck, complacent, or just bored creatively, shake things up. For me, this has meant actually picking up and moving to LA, London, and Nashville over the years, sometimes with no plan and certainly no plan B. It can be scary, but songwriters are artists and that's what artists do sometimes. They jump into the unknown. Every jump I've ever made has made me a better, more aware songwriter. It's as important to live and experience things as it is to study and practice your craft.

2. **Study the Great Ones.** Like most writers I know, I learned by deconstructing songs. How are they put together? Why do some relate to so many people and become hits? The process of breaking down songs and putting them back together gets in your DNA as a writer and is bound to make you better.

3. **Network.** This can be a hard one for us introverts, but I promise, those connections you make will come back time and time again to be invaluable. I still connect with writers I wrote with twenty years ago. They're great co-writers but, more importantly, great friends, and you need friends to survive in this business.

4. **Be Fearless.** Maybe the best advice I ever got. The best cuts I've ever had came from songs that were written without a "net." If I surprised myself and loved the result, chances are someone else will.

5. **Be a good hang.** You're in it for the long run, and believe it or not, the writing community is smaller than you think. Being prepared, considerate, and a good listener makes you someone people will want to work with again. Word spreads.

*M Magazine* asked me recently to pick my five favorite things about being a songwriter.

1. **Freedom.** Freedom to express yourself, freedom to write what you sometimes can't say, freedom to travel, freedom from nine to five. This is one you have to earn through hard work and determination, but you know that already. No one pays you in the beginning.

2. **Relationships.** Most every great friendship in my life has been a direct or indirect result of my pursuit of a song-writing career.

3. **Travel.** Music can open you up to the world. Co-writing with artists and other writers has taken me to places I never could have imagined growing up in Syracuse. I've written in castles in France, hotels in New York, studios in Los Angeles, Music Row in Nashville, Paris, Stockholm, and more.

4. **The buzz.** For me, it never gets better than that moment you feel like you're doing exactly what God put you on the earth to do. You don't know how you got from that spark of inspiration to hearing your song get out into the world and from there, maybe it inspires someone else. That's a perfect buzz.

5. **Character.** I struggled to find a way to explain this, but here are a few thoughts. Facing a blank page, trying to conjure up some magic, dealing with an enormous amount of rejection, trying to stay afloat, stay current

and relevant, keep friendships, marriages, and a roof over your head while you try to focus and keep your head on straight after some success, then doing it again and again . . . you better believe this will build some character over time.

**Sooner or later** someone will ask you what you do for a living. You say, "I'm a songwriter." They say, "Have you written anything I know?" God help you if you can't rattle off a few hits. You might even be tempted to think, "Maybe I'm not really a songwriter," but don't go there. Please. If you've written a song, you're a songwriter. Plain and simple.

There will be more people telling you you're crazy, self-centered, and maybe irresponsible in the beginning. People can be cruel and sometimes jealous along the way. Truth is, you don't need those people. There are plenty of like-minded souls to help you on your path. Seek them out at every turn. If you're focused only on security, money, or stardom, you're in for a rough ride.

Songwriting doesn't have to be life and death, but if you want to do this for life, then treat it with respect and work at it every day. It will reward you beyond measure.

**It's your career, and no one is going to care about your career like you do.**

**Old friends. Photo by Tom Hooke.**

# THE END OF THE ROAD

Spent the afternoon with my old friend Kye Fleming. We have a history of co-writing, and even though it's been a few years since we've written together, our conversation always comes around to why it worked so well for us. It was always easy, but it was more than that. We shared the same spirit when it came to songwriting—it's meant to be fun!

Sure, you need to have drive to get your songs heard, but letting go of the wheel when you write and just seeing where the journey takes you is the deal. Those are the trips we remembered.

I talk with more and more writers who approach writing like the dad in the vacation-from-hell stories. All about the destination. Plan out every detail, quickest and most predictable route, no unscheduled pit stops, hold it as long as you can (OK, maybe that was just my memory). God forbid we get lost, and let's just get there safe and sound. Safe and sound scares me. I've written my share of safe-and-sound songs. But I honestly can't remember them. I remember every one where I just got lost. With songwriters I coach, I'm hoping I can help them learn to drive so they'll throw away the map, roll the windows down, and enjoy the ride.

I have the same wish for you. Whether you write on your own or with co-writers, I hope you have so much fun that you look up and realize you got there but don't know how. It's all about the song journey.

**"**

**Letting go of the wheel when you write and just seeing where the journey takes you is the deal.**

**"**

# ACKNOWLEDGMENTS

I want to thank all the songwriters who have shared their talents with me, helped me learn this craft, and have this life of a songwriter.

The guys I did the early miles with in Binghamton, New York: Dave Bohush, Pete Davis, Nick Marcy, Vinnie Malacarne, Jack Graham, Bucky Dobell, and Charlie Solak. The Zampi brothers, Gina, Alfie and Angie, Jim Rose, my mom and dad, my brothers, Tom, Bob, and especially Jack, for bringing home the first guitar I ever laid eyes on.

Indiana years: Thanks to Carl, Barnsey, Johnny C and Bennie, Coop, Joe Halderman, Wille and Martha Faust, Mike and Jacque Griffen, Bobby Fox, Terry Barnes, Bill Brunt, Alan Johnson, Greg Riker, Jeff Gardner, Stu Berk, Bill Baker, Ron Townsend, Doug Baab, Ron Below, Dane Clark, Roadmaster, Dan Kastings, Jay Koons and Stephanie, Judy Brown Gates, Craig Pinkus, Kristi Lee, Peggy Egan, Phyllis Reynolds, Tom Griswold, The Bob and Tom Show, and every act I shared a stage with along with every crew member and club owner in the Hoosier days. Also want to thank Kathy's folks, Floyd and Marjorie, for letting their Midwest daughter run away with a music guy.

In the LA years: Bill Wray, John Frankenheimer, Rebel Steiner, Clyde Lieberman, Virgin Songs, Mike Murphy, Kirk Butler, Bob and Julie Terry, Dave Kelly, Bob Davis, Jonathan Stone, Evan

Meadow and Debbie Dill at Windswept Pacific, Miles Copeland, Stephan Oberhoff, and the amazing Brenda Russell.

London for being my second home: Eliot Kennedy, Nick Battle, Bob Grace, Lulu and Billy Lawrie, Kipper, Martin Barter, Torquil Creevy, Restless Johnny, Billy Gaff and the Marquee, the Ship, David Stark and SongLink International, Martin Sutton, and the Songwriting Academy.

Nashville, home these last twenty-four years: Way too many to name but most especially Kye Fleming, Tony Brown, Wynonna Judd, Bob and Etta Britt, Chris Ogelsby, Mary Ann Kennedy, Shelby Kennedy, Steve Markland, Leslie Tomasina Dipiero, Bill McDermott, Ed and Laura Hill, GraceWorks, and every session player and artist who's recorded my songs here. Without a doubt, it's Music City.

John and Jo Ann Braheny, Ian and Joanie Crombie and the West Coast Songwriters Association, the Australian Songwriters Association, Mike Ross and Bob Bailey at Sweetwater Music. *Songwriting Magazine UK*, Ira Greenfield and the USA Songwriting Competition, Alan John and the UK Songwriting Contest, and Belmont University.

For giving me the support to coach others: Bobby Harrington, Joe and Alice Beam, Ted Cornelius, Tony and Kathy Dupree, Mick Evans, Jayne Sachs, Tom Nichols, and Tom and Jane Farr. A special thanks to my friend Terry Brown for sharing the miles with me. I've dedicated this book to my wife Kathy and our family, but want to thank them once again for being a constant source of inspiration and joy.

I want to thank Tucker Max and all the following at Scribe Media in Austin Texas for helping bring my book into focus:

- Editing: Hal Clifford
- Proofreading: Brannan Sirratt, Sheila Trask, Joyce Li, Areil Sutton
- Copywriting: Josh Raymer
- Cover and Graphics: Cindy Curtis, Erin Tyler, Alex Robbins
- Layout Design: Derek George
- Publishing Coordinator: Rae Williams
- Publishing Manager: Diana Fitts
- Marketing: Zach Obront, Jesse Sussman

All of my songwriting clients around the world with iDoCoach: You've all become friends along the way, and I'm beyond grateful for your trust.

Lastly, to everyone who's offered me friendship, encouragement, and love along the way, thank you and God bless. As John Lennon said:

*Some are dead and some are living; in my life, I've loved them all.*

# ABOUT THE AUTHOR

Mark Cawley is a hit US songwriter and musician who coaches other writers and artists to reach their creative and professional goals. To date, his songs have been on more than sixteen million records. During his decades in the music business, he has procured cuts with artists ranging from Tina Turner, Joe Cocker, Chaka Khan, and Diana Ross to Wynonna Judd, Kathy Mattea, Russ Taff, Paul Carrack, Will Downing, Tom Scott, Billie Piper, Pop Idol winners, and the Spice Girls.

Mark's résumé includes hits on the pop, country, R&B, jazz, and rock charts and publishing deals with Virgin, Windswept Pacific, and Steelworks/Universal. He has been a co-writer with Eliot Kennedy, Burt Bacharach, Simon Climie, and Kye Fleming, among many others. He is a judge for the UK Songwriting Contest, Nashville Rising Star, Belmont University's Commercial Music program, and West Coast Songwriter events; a contributing author to *USA Songwriting* and *Songwriter Magazine*; a sponsor for the Australian Songwriting Association; mentor for the Songwriting Academy UK; and a popular blogger at www.idocoach.com.

He is a coach and mentor for songwriter clients around the globe through his one-on-one online coaching service, iDoCoach.

Born in Syracuse, New York, Mark has lived in Boston, LA, Indianapolis, London, and for the last twenty-four years, Nashville, Tennessee.

44084254R00126

Made in the USA
Lexington, KY
06 July 2019